MONOGRAPHS OF
SOCIETY FOR RESEARCH IN
CHILD DEVELOPMENT

Serial No. 231, Vol. 58, No. 1, 1993

YOUNG CHILDREN'S UNDERSTANDING OF PRETENSE

Paul L. Harris
Robert D. Kavanaugh

WITH COMMENTARY BY
Henry M. Wellman and
Anne K. Hickling

AND A REPLY BY THE AUTHORS

MONOGRAPHS OF THE SOCIETY FOR RESEARCH IN CHILD DEVELOPMENT
Serial No. 231, Vol. 58, No. 1, 1993

CONTENTS

ABSTRACT

HARRIS, PAUL L., and KAVANAUGH, ROBERT D. Young Children's Understanding of Pretense. With Commentary by HENRY M. WELLMAN and
ANNE K. HICKLING; and a Reply by PAUL L. HARRIS and ROBERT D.
KAVANAUGH. *Monographs of the Society for Research in Child Development*,
1993, **58**(1, Serial No. 231).

Children's understanding of adult pretense was assessed in seven experiments. By the age of 28 months, children are able to understand when
an adult refers to a make-believe substance, such as "tea" or "cereal": they
appropriately direct their pretend actions to a prop that "contains" the
substance (Experiment 1). Similarly, when an adult introduces a make-
believe substitution (e.g., treats wooden blocks as bananas), children appropriately extrapolate that substitution to new props (Experiment 2). In ac-
knowledging such make-believe identities, children are flexible: they direct
different pretend actions to the same prop depending on the make-believe
identity that is conferred on it by the ongoing pretense episode (Experiments 3 and 4). When they watch an adult transform an imaginary substance by "pouring," "spilling," "squeezing," etc., children can also work out
the causal consequences. They realize, for example, that imaginary tea has
been spilled onto a table or that imaginary toothpaste has been squeezed
onto a make-believe banana. They produce a suitable remedial action (Experiment 5) or describe what has happened with appropriate nonliteral
language (Experiments 6 and 7). A theoretical model is proposed to explain
how children can both construct a coherent mental representation of a
pretense episode and use that representation to guide pretend actions and
language. The model is compared to other proposed accounts of pretense.

I. INTRODUCTION

Children enjoy and participate in pretend play from an early age, but their competence is puzzling. In a pretend tea party, for example, an adult picks up an empty teapot, "pours" tea into a cup, and then hands the child the cup. One might expect a child to be bewildered by such bizarre behavior. After all, the adult's actions are a combination of the familiar and the deviant. The act of pouring is executed in a familiar fashion: the container is held above the receptacle and tilted. Yet this action produces no perceptible consequence: the cup remains conspicuously empty. Nevertheless, the adult behaves as if the normal consequence had occurred. She picks up the cup and hands it to the child—implying that the child should now drink from an empty cup.

In the course of such a tea party, the adult may also produce strange remarks. For example, if the child inadvertently knocks the cup over, the adult might exclaim, "Uh oh, you've spilled your tea. You'd better wipe it up"—even though there is no tea, no spillage, and nothing to wipe up.

Children's willingness to go along with such overtures—to sip from the empty cup or to wipe a perfectly dry table—suggests that they can make sense of what the adult has done and said. They realize that it is pretend tea that has been poured or spilled and that the adult is inviting them to drink or wipe up this imaginary liquid rather than the real thing.

Theoretical interest in pretense has been reawakened by research on the child's understanding of mental states (Astington, Harris, & Olson, 1988). Pretend actions have certain parallels with actions based on mistaken belief: both may be directed at situations that do not actually obtain. As noted earlier, someone participating in a pretend tea party might act as if an empty teapot contained tea. By the age of 4 or 5 years, children also understand how "serious" actions may be directed at situations that do not actually obtain. For example, they appreciate that someone who falsely believes that there is a desirable object in a container may make the mistake of searching there (Avis & Harris, 1991; Wimmer & Perner, 1983).

Given such parallels, it has been argued that there are important links between the cognitive processes needed to understand pretense and false beliefs (Leslie, 1987). Consistent with that claim, many autistic children do show impairments in understanding false beliefs (Baron-Cohen, Leslie, & Frith, 1985) and poverty in their spontaneous pretend play (Harris, in press).

Despite these provocative theoretical proposals, our current empirical picture suffers from an important gap. We have a detailed picture of the child's developing understanding of belief (Perner, 1991; Wellman, 1990). Also, thanks to the research that built on Piaget's observations of pretend play, we have a rich account of children's production of pretense in the second and third years of life. Yet we know very little about children's understanding of another person's pretense. In this *Monograph,* we begin to analyze the scope of that comprehension process, to infer the cognitive mechanisms that underlie it, and to consider its implications for current theories of early symbolic abilities.

Comprehension can be analyzed at several levels. First, we may ask whether children understand the *content* of the other person's pretend gestures and remarks. For example, in the episode described above, the child needs to appreciate that the adult is not simply tilting an empty teapot in the air but rather "pouring" pretend tea; when the adult goes on to refer to "tea" being "spilled," the child should realize that pretend tea is being referred to, not genuine tea; and when the cup is knocked over, the child should apply an understanding of liquid displacement to infer the consequences for the pretend tea. In sum, understanding of a pretense episode requires that children go beyond a literal encoding of the other person's actions and remarks to construct a coherent representation of their nonliteral content.

At a more inclusive level, we can ask whether children do not simply appreciate the moment-to-moment content of the other person's pretense but also mark that content as falling within a pretense frame or boundary (Bateson, 1972; Bretherton, 1984). Children can signal that boundary with varying degrees of explicitness. They may temporarily drop a pretense role, reverting to their own voice in order to issue prompts to a partner with the clear aim of redirecting the pretense episode. Alternatively, they may make proposals that include such explicit phrases as "Pretend that . . ." or "Let's say . . ." (Giffin, 1984).

Finally, we can ask children to comment on the implications and status of actions, episodes, or premises that fall within the pretense frame. Recent evidence shows that 3–5-year-old children appreciate that pretend entities are not real and cannot be touched or seen (Harris, Brown, Marriott, Whittall, & Harmer, 1991; Wellman & Estes, 1986). They also understand something about the mental or internal origin of such pretend entities or situations, explaining that they exist in a person's "mind/imagination/brain/head" (Dias & Harris, 1990; Estes, Wellman, & Woolley, 1989).

The experiments that we describe focus on the first level: the moment-to-moment decoding of the nonliteral content of an adult's pretend actions and remarks. The child's appropriate and selective responding can often serve as an index of whether the child has understood that nonliteral content. For example, in the episode described earlier, it would be appropriate for the child to pick up a sponge—or a substitute object that might serve as a sponge—and to pretend to wipe tea from the table. A failure of decoding can lead to an inappropriate response. For example, DeLoache and Plaetzer (1985) report an incident similar to the one described, in which the child searched the table for real tea to wipe up and, failing to find any, did not know how to respond.

As we discuss in more detail below, the comprehension of such simple episodes recruits a variety of cognitive processes. First, however, it is useful to review earlier studies of pretending that are pertinent to the issue of comprehension.

THE UNDERSTANDING OF PRETENSE: EARLIER RESEARCH

Piaget's (1951) seminal work had two important consequences for the study of pretense. First, it provided a widely accepted theory of pretending that emphasized (a) the symbolic nature of pretense, (b) the child's ability to differentiate systematically between signifier (e.g., a piece of cloth) and signified (e.g., a pillow), and (c) the iconic relation (i.e., based on perceptual similarity) between signifier and signified as contrasted with the arbitrary relation that is typically found in language. In addition, it inspired a series of influential studies that have provided a solid empirical description of children's production of pretend actions during the course of solitary play. These findings have been systematically reviewed (e.g., Bretherton, 1984; Fein, 1981; McCune-Nicolich & Fenson, 1984; Nicolich, 1977), and we shall not go over the same ground. Instead, we concentrate on more recent studies of play in a social context where the issue of comprehension looms larger.

If the other person is to be a genuine partner in joint pretend play, the child must decode the other's nonliteral actions and remarks since their underlying meaning will not fully coincide with their surface features. A child who understands what the partner intends to convey can begin to engage in the drama and excitement of joint pretense, in which one partner's make-believe builds on and even transforms the make-believe suppositions that have been introduced by the other partner. Seen in this way, the

3

comprehension of pretense is a critical cognitive process in the emergence of genuinely collaborative pretend play.

Recently, several different concerns have increased interest in children's ability to engage in play in a social context. First, a revival of the Vygotskian perspective has led to the argument that play that is either guided or modeled by an adult may be more complex than solitary play (Bretherton, O'Connell, Shore, & Bates, 1984; Fenson, 1984; O'Connell & Bretherton, 1984). Second, as Piaget conceded, more sophisticated forms of pretend play are often collaborative: instead of simply producing a pretend action, children adopt a pretend role (e.g., mother or doctor) that calls for a partner to take on a complementary role (e.g., child or patient) (Dunn & Dale, 1984; Howes, Unger, & Seidner, 1989; Miller & Garvey, 1984). Third, attachment theorists have begun to see the child's pretend play as an index of the relationship between caretaker and child (Slade, 1987a, 1987b). Accordingly, for a variety of reasons, investigators have started to focus on children's pretend play in a social context, that is, when a partner—be it an unfamiliar adult, a familiar caretaker, a sibling, or a peer—is available.

Surprisingly, however, researchers interested in social play have continued to emphasize the production of pretense, not its comprehension. They have compared the frequency and sophistication of pretense production under different social conditions. For example, there is consistent evidence that play is more elaborate and sustained in the presence of a familiar caretaker. In particular, the caretaker's active interventions and suggestions, rather than her mere presence, augment pretend play by 1- and 2-year-olds (DeLoache & Plaetzer, 1985; Fiese, 1990; O'Connell & Bretherton, 1984; Slade, 1987a). There is also evidence that modeling by an adult enhances subsequent pretend play as compared with premodeling performance (Bretherton et al., 1984; Fenson, 1984). Despite these robust findings, we have little information about when and how children start to understand a caretaker's pretense. Below, we review these recent studies of pretense in a social context in more detail. We first consider studies in which the child's play is structured by an adult; next, we consider the effects of modeling; finally, we turn to studies of pretend play between children. In each case, our aim is to assess what conclusions can be drawn about the comprehension of pretense.

PRETENSE IN A SOCIAL CONTEXT

Joint Play with an Adult

In several different studies, children's spontaneous pretend play with toys has been compared under two conditions: when the mother is present in the room but otherwise occupied and when she is available to participate in the child's play. One consistent finding is that the availability of the mother augments pretend play. For example, in studies of 20- and 28-month-old infants, O'Connell and Bretherton (1984) observed an increase in the diversity of pretend play at 28 months, while Slade (1987a) observed an increase for both age groups in the overall duration of pretend play, in the duration of the longest episode, in the amount of time spent in preparation or planning (e.g., search for a particular prop), and in the maturity of pretend episodes (as defined by Nicolich, 1977). Fiese (1988, 1990) reported an increase in the frequency of make-believe play for infants ranging from 15 to 36 months when the mother was available as a partner.

Mothers can influence play in a direct fashion, by making suggestions that children follow or by demonstrating an activity that children mimic (Kavanaugh & Harris, 1991; O'Connell & Bretherton, 1984). However, mothers do not necessarily inspire children by supplying an initial idea for a make-believe episode; their participation is also effective for episodes that children initiate themselves (Kavanaugh, Whittington, & Cerbone, 1983; Slade, 1987a). In fact, although the mother's involvement usually facilitates pretend play, it can sometimes be disruptive if mothers intrude with questions or new activities (Fiese, 1990). Moreover, mothers vary in the way that they make themselves available. Thus, in comparison with mothers of insecurely attached infants, mothers of securely attached infants participated more in their child's play, and their infants responded to such participation, especially interactive involvement rather than verbal commentary, by producing longer and more mature make-believe episodes (Slade, 1987a, 1987b).

These studies clearly show that the mother's participation can increase the duration and maturity of make-believe play provided that it does not become intrusive. Yet they permit no firm conclusions about whether children understand the content of their caretaker's pretense. As one prototypical example, consider a mother who sips from an empty cup and then invites her child to "give Dolly some juice." It is tempting to conclude that a child who takes up this suggestion and holds a cup to the doll's mouth has understood that the mother was pretending to drink and that her request refers to pretend juice rather than real juice. On the other hand, a simpler interpretation is available. The child may have been cued to enact a pretend script simply by the provision of appropriate props or by the mother's demonstration. Watching mother sip from the cup, or simply being handed a cup, might prompt the child to pretend to give the doll a drink, whether or not the child understands the mother's pretense. More generally, a mother who knows her child's pretense repertoire might successfully elicit pretense by cuing the child to act on (or search for) a particular prop. Nothing in the results of studies to date rules out this interpretation.

Indeed, observational evidence confirms that caretakers do attempt to structure a child's pretense by supplying appropriate cues. Miller and Garvey (1984) report that, when mothers encouraged 2-year-olds to engage in pretend, they "arranged the situation in which such play took place and provided props, including toy replicas of clothing, dishes, bottles and so on" (p. 115). This kind of maternal scaffolding means that children may complement their partner's pretense without understanding what their partner is pretending to do. For example, Miller and Garvey (1984) describe an extended episode between Beth, aged 29 months, and her mother, who exchanged mother-child roles. Seeing that Beth was pretending to cook, the mother supplied various additional cues: she referred to Beth as "Mommy," and she announced that she herself was hungry, proffering a spoon and asking to be fed. Beth in turn pretended to cook and to feed her mother. Although she may have understood that her mother was pretending to be a baby, Beth's pretend actions could also have been carried out in the absence of that understanding. As Miller and Garvey point out, children's mothering is an elaboration of doll-directed play that emerges in the second year. Thus, Beth may have treated her mother as a more flexible and responsive partner than a doll, incorporating her into the familiar mothering script with no recognition that the mother was simultaneously pretending to be a baby.

Questions about what the young child actually understands are raised in one of the few studies to look explicitly at the child's comprehension of the mother's pretense. DeLoache and Plaetzer (1985) confirmed that children ranging from 15 to 30 months produced more sophisticated make-believe play when the mother was available as a partner. Despite this facilitation, there were indications that the toddlers sometimes treated their mothers' contributions literally, rather than incorporating them within the make-believe framework. For example, during a tea party, a 30-month-old boy dropped the sponge and knocked his cup over. His mother responded by saying, "Oh-oh, you spilled your tea. You better wipe it up." The child picked up the sponge and scrutinized the area surrounding the cup, asking, "Where?" DeLoache and Plaetzer comment that he appeared to be searching for real tea, not pretend tea. Moreover, 25% of their subjects provided clear examples of such apparent shifts from a pretend to a literal or reality mode. Because children are likely to ignore what they do not understand, this proportion is probably a conservative estimate of their comprehension failures.

The Effects of Modeling

When children watch an adult enact a pretend episode, they often reproduce some of the adult's pretend actions in subsequent play. To assess this priming effect experimentally, investigators have compared children's pretend play before and after the modeling of pretend actions by an adult. For example, Fenson (1984) observed that, after an adult had modeled a pretense episode, object substitutions were more frequent and widespread among 26-month-olds; other-directed pretend actions and the invention of imaginary objects were more frequent and widespread among 31-month-olds. Bretherton et al. (1984) found that modeling, particularly with realistic props, led to an increase in pretend actions and utterances among 20- and 28-month-olds.

Modeling effects have also been observed among younger children. Watson and Fischer (1977) found that, during an initial familiarization phase, infants (ranging from 14 to 24 months) produced none of the pretend actions that were subsequently modeled but that most did so after modeling. Similarly, Fenson and Ramsay (1981) found that 19-month-olds, and to a lesser extent 15-month-olds, produced more two-part actions (e.g., the doll is placed in a lying position and then covered with a cloth) following modeling.

It might be argued that such modeling effects are based on children's comprehension of the model's pretend actions and utterances. If that argument is correct, then modeling effects would provide a useful measure of children's comprehension: to the extent that children reproduce a model's pretend actions, they have understood them. However, there are three objections to this proposal. First, it is unlikely that comprehension is always a prerequisite for imitation. For example, in the case of language, children can, within limits, reproduce utterances that they do not understand (Fraser, Bellugi, & Brown, 1963). In the case of actions and gestures, they can reproduce simple movements before 12 months and even, arguably, at birth (Meltzoff, 1988; Meltzoff & Moore, 1983). Thus, although it is likely that the comprehension of a pretend sequence facilitates accurate reproduction, we cannot assume that comprehension is necessary. The child's capacity for simple motor imitation may enable a child to copy a pretend action with no understanding of its nonliteral meaning.

The second objection concerns the type of comprehension required for accurate reproduction. When an adult models a pretend sequence with objects, the child might understand it as an integrated sequence based on pretend attributes of the objects or, alternatively, as an integrated sequence based on literal properties of the objects. Consider the sequence mentioned earlier: an adult places a doll in a lying position and covers it with a cloth. A child might interpret this as a pretend sequence: the doll is placed in a "sleeping" position before being covered by a "blanket." Alternatively, the child might interpret this as a literal sequence: the doll is placed in a convenient horizontal position before being covered by the cloth. Accurate reproduction might be facilitated by either type of comprehension. Notice, moreover, that both types of comprehension are likely to improve with age; one cannot therefore determine which is operative simply by showing that modeling effects are more pronounced among older children.

The final objection to using modeling effects as an index of comprehension concerns the danger of false negatives rather than false positives. Bretherton et al. (1984) observed that, after watching an adult enact an episode involving a mother bear as agent and a baby bear as patient, 20-month-olds frequently simplified the episode when they reenacted it: they tended to assign both bears to the patient role. By contrast, 28-month-olds were much more likely to preserve the active role of the mother bear. One interpretation is that the younger group failed to understand the mother's role. An equally plausible interpretation, however, is that the younger group understood her role but could not reenact it.

In sum, although modeling effects suggest that children can understand an adult's pretend actions and utterances, they may overestimate or underestimate that ability.

Joint Play with Other Children

Joint play with a sibling has a different complexion than joint play with the mother. Mothers often participate through verbal commentary alone, supplemented by reference to a toy or prop. By contrast, siblings participate more as actors than as commentators, and they often call for a change of role, psychological state, or location, with less reliance on props (Dale, 1989; Dunn & Dale, 1984).

Investigators do not agree on the age at which collaborative role play emerges. For example, Miller and Garvey (1984) claim that clear instances are seen only in the fourth year, whereas Howes et al. (1989) report cooperative role play in the middle of the third year (around 29–33 months). Dunn and Dale (1984) even report selected examples among 2-year-olds (aged 24 months).

The examples provided by Dunn and Dale are especially provocative because they offer enough detail to make a preliminary assessment of whether 2-year-olds grasp that their sibling is pretending. For example, when Richard's sister tells him, "The train's got stuck," and asks him to supply more petrol, Richard responds by pretending to supply petrol and making a suitable "Sssssss" sound as he does so. When Laura's sister adopts the role of baby and asks Laura to put some cream on, Laura responds, "Come on Baby. I put some cream on. Get in (pretend bed) . . . (gives 'food')" (Dunn & Dale, 1984, p. 141, exx. 1 and 2, respectively). In these two examples, the older sibling introduces a pretend substance or identity—either through explicit naming, as in the case of petrol, or through enactment, as in the case of the role of baby. The younger (24-month-old) sibling then produces an action or comment that acknowledges this pretense. Thus, Richard supplies imaginary petrol, marking its delivery with appropriate sounds, and Laura explicitly refers to her sister's temporary pretend identity.

However, it is difficult to assess how far these intriguing examples represent the competence of the average 2-year-old. They may reflect only the ability of more advanced 2-year-olds since Dunn and Dale point out that, in two different studies, collaborative role play between siblings was observed in only 20% and 33% of their samples.

Summary and Conclusions

There is consistent evidence from several different laboratories that toddlers' pretend play is more sophisticated when their caretaker is available as a play partner. Although this facilitation might be interpreted as evidence that toddlers understand their mothers' pretense overtures, it is also possible that toddlers benefit chiefly from the props, demonstrations, and cues that mothers supply. Indeed, positive signs of misunderstanding have been observed.

Children also engage in more sophisticated play after watching an adult engage in pretense. However, such postmodeling effects provide an equivocal index of children's comprehension. They might copy an adult's pretend action with no understanding of its nonliteral meaning; alternatively, they may understand that nonliteral meaning but have difficulty reenacting it.

Collaborative role play between children implies not only the complementary production of pretense but also mutual comprehension. The analysis of such collaborative play has only just begun, and investigators disagree about the age at which it emerges. Detailed transcripts provided by Dunn and Dale (1984) suggest that some 24-month-olds can understand an older sibling's pretense initiative, but such competence may not be representative.

THE NATURE OF PRETENSE COMPREHENSION

We may now consider in more detail how children might display an understanding of the content of their partner's pretense. Our discussion will examine four interrelated facets of comprehension. (1) Children who understand a make-believe stipulation should be able to display their comprehension by responding to that stipulation appropriately and extrapolating where appropriate to new instances. (2) They should be able to generate novel pretend actions tailored to the make-believe identity of the prop. (3)

Having understood a make-believe stipulation, they should also understand the pretend changes that can be carried out on the imaginary entity or substitute object. (4) Finally, they should be able to talk about such make-believe changes. Below, we consider each of these possibilities in turn, beginning with the notions of stipulation and extrapolation.

Stipulation and Extrapolation of a Make-Believe Identity

Social pretend play often begins with one partner stipulating the make-believe identity of an object or event. This can be achieved in two different ways (Bretherton, 1984; Garvey, 1984; Schwartzmann, 1978). A partner may briefly step outside the play framework by making an explicit statement about the make-believe status of an object. For example, during joint play, a mother may point to a prop and say, "Let's pretend this is cheese." Alternatively, a partner can remain within the play framework by designating the pretend identity of a prop implicitly, that is, by acting on, or talking about, its make-believe qualities. Thus, a mother might ask for a "piece of cheese" in the presence of a prop that bears some degree of resemblance to the real object. The latter strategy is risky, particularly with young children, who may fail to understand the pretense supposition of the partner. Nevertheless, there is evidence that, even in joint play with infants, implicit reference dominates. For example, Kavanaugh and Harris (1991) found that, in dyadic play with 18–24-month-olds, mothers often made verbal requests that relied solely on implicit reference. Thus, mothers presumed an understanding of make-believe food, such as a hot dog, by requesting it by name in the presence of an appropriate prop, or they implied that milk existed by asking for it in the presence of an empty milk carton. They did not feel compelled to step outside the play framework, by pointing to an object and explicitly identifying its make-believe characteristics, even when the pretend entity (e.g., milk) was represented only indirectly by a supporting prop (e.g., an empty milk carton). Thus, a good deal of pretense knowledge was assumed in these joint interactions. Unfortunately, these observational data do not show whether children understood their mothers' requests or whether the maternal scaffolding described earlier carried the play forward in the absence of comprehension.

Once it has been stipulated that one object is to act "as if" it were another, this make-believe substitution can be extended to other available exemplars. Such extrapolation is a particularly crucial feature of make-believe since, as Walton (1990) points out, it provides a basis for discovering rather than just inventing make-believe truths. For illustrative purposes, we may borrow an example from Walton (1990). Two children playing in the woods agree that tree stumps are to count as bears; once they agree, it follows that any stump in the vicinity—even one that the children have not yet seen—is, fictionally speaking, a bear. If a thicket hides a stump, then there is a "bear" awaiting discovery by the children. As Walton points out, such fictional truths may be quite independent of the imagination of the partners, at least temporarily. A concealed stump is a "bear" whether or not either child has spotted it. More generally, if partners can engage in a process of extrapolation, they can explore the make-believe worlds that they create, and these worlds can contain surprises. They are not simply a predictable and transparent product of the partners' imagination.

Pretend Actions Based on a Make-Believe Identity

The stipulation of a make-believe identity is a fundamental component of pretense comprehension because it allows new entities to be incorporated into joint play. Studies of joint play suggest that partners not only stipulate the existence of a make-believe entity but also expect their partner to produce pretend actions that respect that identity. For example, in research with both mother-child (Kavanaugh & Harris, 1991) and sibling (Dunn & Dale, 1984) dyads, the child partner was called on to engage in a different pretend action depending on the make-believe entity that had been introduced. A mother might say, "Do we have any milk to drink?" while holding out a glass (Kavanaugh & Harris, 1991). In the example cited earlier, Richard's sister asked him to supply imaginary petrol because the train was stuck (Dunn & Dale, 1984). Thus, the partner was expected to pour imaginary milk from a container into a cup or to pump imaginary petrol into the train. Sometimes, the same prop may even assume two successive and different identities depending on the pretend episode in progress. For example, a cushion may stand for a gate and then for a tunnel (Dunn & Dale, 1984, ex. 1). In such cases, the children must tailor their pretend actions to the object's current stipulated identity.

Causal Transformation of a Make-Believe Entity

Recall DeLoache and Plaetzer's (1985) observation of a mother who deviated from the canonical tea-party script by suggesting that the child had spilled make-believe tea. Whereas tea is normally transferred from teapot to cup to mouth, this mother drew attention to the causal effect of knocking over a cup. As the child's confused response showed, such a pretend transformation is not likely to be understood simply by reference to what normally happens at tea parties. Rather, it needs to be appreciated in terms of the more wide-ranging causal principles concerning support, containment, and liquid displacement that children typically master during the sensorimotor period. However, the special feature of such nonliteral transformations is that they afford little perceptual feedback with which to decode what has happened. The child must infer the causal transformation by tracking the movement of props associated with the imaginary substance, for example, the container. Thus, from seeing the objectively empty cup knocked over, the child must work out that a transformation of the make-believe tea inside it has occurred: it has been spilled onto the table.[1]

Although the child observed by DeLoache and Plaetzer (1985) failed to infer what transformation had occurred, other evidence is more encouraging. Miller and Garvey (1984) report that a 29-month-old did successfully wipe up the (pretend) mess after her mother had pretended to spill milk. Leslie (1988a) briefly reports a more structured study with 2-year-olds who were encouraged to join in and comment on a game of pretense led by the experimenter. In the course of the game, the experimenter enacted various pretend sequences. For example, pretend water was scooped out of a bath into a cup or tipped out of a cup over a toy animal. No quantitative analysis is given, but Leslie notes that children of around 30 months usually kept track of these changes. For example, they said that the cup contained "water," or refilled it when it was empty, or realized that the toy animal was "wet." These intriguing results clearly imply that some 2-year-olds do understand make-believe transformations.

Describing Make-Believe Transformations

Children who watch and understand a pretend transformation, such as tea being spilled, could demonstrate their comprehension by describing what has happened. However, there has been little study of children's pretend language, during either the production or the comprehension of pretense.

Young children's language is often described as restricted to the here and now. This characterization implies that children will have difficulty describing make-believe events. Admittedly, such events are often enacted in front of the child and thus may appear to resemble ordinary here-and-now activities. However, as noted above, a full description of a make-believe event involves several distinct mental processes. To return to our example of spilled tea, when a teacup is knocked over, the imaginary outcome is richer than the perceived event. Accordingly, a verbal account of the make-believe consequences of this outcome needs to go beyond a literal description. The child must refer to an imaginary substance (e.g., "tea") and an

---

[1] Note that we use the term "transformation" to refer to changes that occur within the pretend world, such as tea being poured or spilled; we do not wish to invoke the more technical usage introduced by Fein (1975).

imaginary outcome (e.g., "wet"), not simply to the teacup falling over. Such pretend entities and attributes do not exist in the here and now, however obvious they may be to a sophisticated play partner.

It is interesting to note that, in one of the few studies of children's pretend language, Fenson (1984) reported that 2-year-olds sometimes produced a verbal description of make-believe episodes or actions: they referred to substitute or imaginary objects in terms of their make-believe identity. These utterances were not common at 20 months, but they were quite widespread among 28-month-olds, especially in a postmodeling phase (Fenson, 1984, table 4). Bretherton and her colleagues (Bretherton et al., 1984) observed a similar sharp increment in pretend language between 20 and 28 months. These observations suggest that 2-year-olds may be able to understand a play partner's pretense and then describe it in their own words.

PLAN OF THE STUDY

Seven experiments were designed to explore these various aspects of pretense comprehension. All the experiments included 2-year-olds. Depending on the particular study, children younger than 2 years were also included.

In Experiment 1, children were required to respond to the stipulation of a make-believe identity (e.g., "tea") by selecting appropriately between two different associated props. The critical question was whether children would choose an associated prop (e.g., an empty teapot rather than an empty cereal box) on the basis of the imaginary entity stipulated by the experimenter.

Experiment 2 extended the design of Experiment 1 in two important ways. First, the available props (yellow and red bricks) served as substitutes for the make-believe entities ("bananas" and "cakes"), not as associates. Second, children's comprehension was assessed in terms of their ability to extrapolate the stipulated identity in a selective fashion to hitherto unused props.

The young child's ability to produce actions based on a stipulated make-believe identity was examined in Experiments 3 and 4. Children were called on to produce a novel action that was appropriate to the make-believe identity of a prop. To receive credit, children needed (a) to appreciate the implied make-believe identity of the prop (e.g., to realize that a piece of paper could serve as a make-believe towel) and (b) to produce a novel action appropriate to that make-believe identity (e.g., "drying" a teddy bear). To ensure that children were not simply cued by the prop, independent of the experimenter's make-believe script, each prop was embedded in two

13

different scripts that called for distinct actions (e.g., a piece of paper served as a make-believe towel in one script and as a make-believe pillow in the other).

Experiments 1–4 established at what age and under what conditions children understand make-believe stipulations and pretend in agreement with them. These data provided an appropriate foundation for Experiment 5, which focused on whether children also understand the transformations that a make-believe entity can undergo, such as spilling, wetting, and so forth. Children were shown a make-believe transformation (e.g., make-believe toothpaste being squirted by Teddy onto the tail of an animal). The experimenter invited the child to wipe the animal who was "all dirty." The child could identify the correct animal only by appropriately interpreting the unexpected but causally determined outcome of Teddy's action.

The transformations used in Experiment 5 were deliberately chosen to be partially familiar to the child, but they were also intended to include an unusual outcome. Thus, in the example just described, Teddy acted on a familiar container (e.g., a tube of toothpaste) in a standard fashion. However, although the container and the pretend action were familiar, the pretend outcome was not: animals do not usually end up with toothpaste on their tails. This meant that children could not respond to the experimenter's request by carrying out the next action in a well-rehearsed script (e.g., brushing the animal's teeth). They could receive credit only if they adjusted their pretend reaction to the implied causal sequence.

In the final two experiments, we asked whether young children could also translate their understanding of such pretend transformations into words. Could they, for example, refer appropriately to an imaginary substance or an imaginary outcome when describing a make-believe transformation? A positive result would reinforce the claim that children can keep track of the make-believe changes that may be acted out during a pretend episode. In addition, it would show that early language need not be confined to a description of actual events, whether in the present, the past, or the future. To explore this possibility, children again watched "naughty Teddy" behave in a mischievous fashion. However, they were called on to display their comprehension of Teddy's transgressions, not by coming to the aid of his victim, but by describing what had happened. A full description of Teddy's actions in Experiments 6 and 7 called for a reference to an imaginary substance and an imaginary outcome. Experiment 7 required, in addition, an appropriate reference to a substitute object.

We anticipated that children who understood their partner's pretense actions would respond selectively and appropriately in the various experiments. This would provide firm evidence that, when children enter into a game of make-believe with a play partner, they are not simply prompted by the available props to produce pretend actions that happen to coincide with the script being enacted. Instead, they use the actions and remarks of the partner to construct a representation of the nonliteral content of the pretend episode.

Having established that young children are capable of constructing such a nonliteral representation, we shall return to the issue raised at the outset. An adult engaged in pretend play with a child produces actions or remarks that are aberrant if they are treated in a literal fashion. By what cognitive process does a child arrive at an appropriate nonliteral interpretation of the pretend overtures of a play partner? Are such processes used in understanding actions and remarks outside the domain of pretend play?

II. UNDERSTANDING MAKE-BELIEVE STIPULATIONS

The stipulation of a make-believe identity can occur in different ways. One of the simplest is for a player to refer to an imaginary entity that is associated with an available prop. Alternatively, a player can refer to a substitute object in terms of its make-believe rather than its literal identity. Either of these two types of pretense initiative can be accompanied by pretend actions, appropriate to the make-believe entity. For example, a player might ask for make-believe tea while at the same time holding out an empty teacup or refer to a substitute object as "cake" while pretending to eat it.

A partner who observes and comprehends such initiatives is in a position to do several things: to select between props in terms of their make-believe identity; to extrapolate a make-believe substitution to similar props in the immediate vicinity; to direct actions toward a prop in terms of its fictional identity; to grasp subsequent transformations of the make-believe entity; to talk about a substitute object or imaginary object in terms of its fictional identity and effects; and so forth. Experiment 1 was designed to look at the first of these abilities—appropriate selection between props.

EXPERIMENT 1

This experiment served as an analogue to a commonly occurring situation in joint play when one partner makes a pretend request of the other. For example, during a tea party between mother and child, a mother may hold out her cup and ask for some tea. A child who correctly interprets this make-believe stipulation is likely to pick up a teapot and simulate pouring tea into her mother's cup. In Experiment 1, we looked for evidence of pretense comprehension among children ranging from 18 to 30 months.

It is important to note, however, that a child who acts appropriately following this kind of request has not necessarily understood the adult's stipulation. This is of particular concern when an adult's request is tailored to the available props, as it normally would be in free play. For example, following their mother's request for "tea," children might pick up a teapot and tip it in a pretend pouring gesture simply because it is the most salient prop on which to act, not because they understand their mother's request.

To rule out this possibility, we used a design in which two different sets of props were simultaneously available: a cup and teapot on one side of the child and a bowl, spoon, and cereal box on the other side. The experimenter then invited the child to feed a set of animals with either imaginary tea or imaginary cereal. Thus, children were required to select appropriately between the two sets of props depending on the particular make-believe stipulation of the adult.

Method

Subjects

In Experiment 1 and in the four succeeding experiments, a group of older 1-year-olds (18–24 months) was compared with younger 2-year-olds (25–31 months). In Experiments 6–7, which called for a verbal response, younger 2-year-olds (24–31 months) were compared with older 2-year-olds (31–36 months). Table 1 shows the gender composition of each age group, the exact age range, and the mean age for each experiment.

The children were tested by a female undergraduate or research assistant. Aside from occasional home testing, testing was carried out in 15 different day-care centers, home-care centers, and play groups located in different areas of the city of Oxford, England. Children in each experiment came from both lower- and middle-class neighborhoods. Most children were Caucasian (90% or more in each experiment). The remainder came from Asian or African families. Irrespective of family background, all children spoke and were tested in English.

Developmental studies of joint pretense have reported no consistent gender differences (Bretherton et al., 1984; Fenson, 1984; Fiese, 1990; O'Connell & Bretherton, 1984). Our earlier exploratory studies also failed to reveal any gender differences (Harris, Kavanaugh, & Walker-Andrews, 1990). Accordingly, no attempt was made to assess the effect of gender in the studies to be reported. Nevertheless, care was taken to choose gender-neutral themes.

Procedure

The experiment was divided into a warm-up phase and an experimental phase; the aim of the former was to encourage children to participate in a game of pretend that involved feeding animals.

TABLE 1

OVERVIEW OF SUBJECTS IN EXPERIMENTS 1–7

EXPERIMENT	YOUNGER THAN 2 YEARS					YOUNGER 2-YEAR-OLDS					OLDER 2-YEAR-OLDS				
	Boys	Girls	Total	Age Range	Mean Age	Boys	Girls	Total	Age Range	Mean Age	Boys	Girls	Total	Age Range	Mean Age
1	12	4	16	18–24	22	10	6	16	25–30	27	…	…	…	…	…
2	9	6	15	19–23	21	9	6	15	25–33	28	…	…	…	…	…
3	8	4	12	17–24	21	9	3	12	25–30	28	…	…	…	…	…
4	10	5	15	18–24	22	7	8	15	25–31	28	…	…	…	…	…
5	6	9	15	18–24	20	9	6	15	25–30	28	…	…	…	…	…
6	…	…	…	…	…	7	9	16	24–31	28	8	8	16	31–36	34
7	…	…	…	…	…	6	5	11	26–31	28	6	5	11	31–35	33

NOTE.—All ages are given in months.

Warm-up phase.—The props for the warm-up phase consisted of an empty milk carton and a glass plus a toy elephant. (The toy elephant and all the other toys used in the experiment represented familiar farmyard or zoo animals. Each was 1–3 inches in height.) The experimenter introduced the toy elephant, saying, "Here's the elephant." The experimenter put the empty glass in front of the elephant and simulated "pouring" milk into it from the empty carton. She then lifted the glass to the elephant's trunk and tilted it, to simulate giving it a drink. Next, children were told, "The elephant wants some more milk. You give the elephant some more milk." The experimenter "poured" more milk into the glass, handed the child the glass, and encouraged him or her to "give the elephant some more milk." The latter phrase was repeated if necessary.

Experimental phase.—The warm-up props were removed and replaced by the experimental props: a cup and an empty teapot were placed on one side of the child and a bowl, a spoon, and an empty cereal box on the other side. Four animals were then introduced one by one in the following order: cow, pig, duck, cat. Each animal was positioned directly in front of the child between the two sets of props. For each animal, the experimenter said, "Here's the ———. The ——— wants some tea/cereal. You give the ——— some tea/cereal." The association of either tea or cereal with each animal had been determined previously by a random shuffle of four cards (two marked "tea" and two marked "cereal"). This procedure ensured that both the order of correct choices and the relation between animals and correct choices were different for each child.

Results

With respect to each of the four test animals, children were scored for two different pretend actions: namely, "pouring" and "feeding." Children received credit for pretend "pouring" if they lifted the empty teapot above the cup and tilted it or lifted the empty cereal box above the bowl and tilted it; they received credit for pretend "feeding" if they lifted the cup or lifted the bowl and/or the spoon toward the animal's mouth. Pretend "pouring" and "feeding" responses were classified as correct or incorrect depending on the experimenter's stipulation of the animal's preference for tea versus cereal. No responses were recorded when the child failed to act on either set of props. Since there were four trials, each calling for two pretend responses (pouring and feeding), correct scores could range from 0 to 8.

Table 2 shows the mean number of correct pourings, correct feedings, incorrect pourings and feedings (these two responses were grouped together since they were infrequent), and no responses. Children in each age group were relatively good at producing both types of correct pretend ac-

TABLE 2

EXPERIMENT 1: MEAN NUMBER OF DIFFERENT TYPES OF RESPONSE
BY YOUNGER (N = 16) AND OLDER (N = 16) CHILDREN

Group	Correct Pouring	Correct Feeding	Incorrect Response	No Response
Younger	1.8	3.3	.3	2.6
	(1.1)	(.8)	(1.0)	(1.3)
Older	3.1	3.8	.3	.8
	(1.1)	(.4)	(.7)	(.8)

NOTE.—Standard deviations are given in parentheses.

tion. Older children typically produced both types of correct action on at least three of the four trials. Younger children were quite good at feeding but often omitted pouring. When correct actions were analyzed with a 2 (age) × 2 (type of action) ANOVA, two reliable findings emerged: older children produced more correct actions than younger children (age, $F[1,30]$ = 15.105, $p < .001$), and children in both groups were more likely to feed with the correct prop than to pour from the correct prop (type of action, $F[1,30]$ = 26.786, $p < .001$). The interaction of age × type of action was close to significance, $F(1,30)$ = 4.05, $p < .06$. Further analysis of this interaction showed that, in comparison to older children, younger children were just as likely to feed from the correct prop, $F(1,60)$ = 2.370, N.S., but less likely to pour from the correct prop, $F(1,60)$ = 17.921, $p < .001$.

The large number of correct actions demonstrated that children were able to choose appropriately between the two sets of props, depending on the experimenter's request to give the animal "tea" or "cereal." In order to check that this selectivity exceeded chance expectation, children were scored for the number of trials (out of four) on which they poured from and/or fed with the correct set of props. Trials on which children made no response or combined a correct pouring with an incorrect feeding (or vice versa) were treated, conservatively, as errors. Table 3 shows the number of children in each age group who made a correct choice on none of the four trials, on one trial, on two trials, on three trials, or on all four trials. A total of 13 younger and 16 older children were correct on more than half the trials (i.e., on either three or four trials). Kolmogorov-Smirnov (two-tailed) tests confirmed that the distribution of subjects differed from chance for both the younger, $D(N = 16)$ = 0.500, $p < .01$, and the older, $D(N = 16)$ = 0.813, $p < .01$, age groups.

Finally, children were very accurate in their choice even on the first experimental trial following the warm-up: 15 of the younger and all 16 older children made a correct choice ($p < .005$ for both age groups, using two-tailed binomial tests).

TABLE 3

EXPERIMENT 1: NUMBER OF YOUNGER ($N = 16$) AND OLDER
($N = 16$) CHILDREN MAKING CORRECT CHOICES ON 0,
1, 2, 3, OR 4 TRIALS

	NUMBER OF CORRECT CHOICES					
GROUP	0	1	2	3	4	MEAN
Younger	0	1	2	5	8	3.25
Older	0	0	0	2	14	3.88

Discussion

On most trials, children fed the animal with the appropriate prop(s). Pouring from the appropriate prop was not frequent in the younger group. Nevertheless, when children were scored in terms of the set of props that they acted on (whether through pouring, feeding, or both), both age groups were highly accurate.

Thus, children guided their pretend response in terms of the make-believe stipulation embedded in the experimenter's request. Performance on the first experimental trial was especially impressive because it immediately followed the warm-up trial, where a different set of props and a different make-believe substance had been referred to. Children in both age groups performed above chance, not just across the set of trials, but also on the first trial. Nonetheless, older children produced more correct responses overall; younger children were especially likely to omit the pouring response. It may be that older children were more alert to the need to fill the cup or bowl before each animal could be fed from it. An equally plausible interpretation, however, is that the younger children were less able to combine the two separate schemas of pouring plus feeding and focused simply on the goal of feeding the animal. In fact, research on the production of pretense has shown that children produce single pretend schemas before being able to combine them (Fenson & Ramsay, 1980; Nicolich, 1977).

Whichever interpretation may be correct, the most important finding is that children aged 18–30 months understood an adult request that stipulated a make-believe substance; that is, they acted as if the make-believe substance were available. It might be argued that children did not realize that the experimenter's request was to supply *pretend* tea or cereal and that, when they lifted the relevant container, they expected to pour *real* tea or cereal. However, appropriate pretend feeding (with the visibly empty cup, bowl, or spoon) was virtually universal, even on Trial 1. Thus, it seems unlikely that children were making a literal response to the experimenter's request and more likely that, primed by the warm-up, they complied in a pretense mode.

EXPERIMENT 2

Here, we examined the child's capacity for identity extrapolation, which provides a basis for discovering rather than just inventing fictional truths (Walton, 1990). Children aged 18–30 months watched while an adult pretended to feed toy animals with a prop representing a particular pretend food. The critical issue was whether they could appropriately extend this pretend identity to unused props in the immediate vicinity.

Method

Subjects

The subjects were 15 older 1-year-olds and 15 younger 2-year-olds (for details, see Table 1 above).

Procedure

Warm-up phase.—Children were seated in front of two separate piles of six yellow and six red bricks; both piles were within easy reach. The bricks were selected for color and shape so as to bear some minimal resemblance to the make-believe entities—bananas and cake, respectively—that they represented. Thus, the yellow bricks were curved (in the form of an arch), and the red bricks were cubes. The experimenter began by introducing a toy monkey, saying, "The monkey wants some banana. Let's give him some banana." Next, the experimenter put a paper plate in front of the monkey, placed a yellow brick on the plate, carried it toward the monkey's head, and made the monkey "eat" the make-believe banana. The child was then handed another yellow brick and told, "The monkey wants some more banana. You give the monkey some more banana," and the child was encouraged to put the yellow brick on the paper plate and make the monkey "eat." The experimenter said, "That's right. The monkey is eating his banana," as the child carried out the appropriate action. The monkey and the two yellow bricks were then placed to one side, but still within easy reach of the child. The experimenter next placed a toy horse in the center facing the paper plate and said, "The horse wants some cake. Let's give him some cake." Except for referring to "cake" and using one of the red bricks, the experimenter then continued exactly as above.

Test phase.—In the test phase, the experimenter introduced four new animals one by one in the following fixed order: cow, pig, duck, cat. For each animal, the experimenter said, "Here's the ———. The ——— wants something to eat." The animal was placed in the center facing the plate (and the child). "The ——— wants some banana/cake. You give the ——— some banana/cake." For each child, the food preference associated with each of the four animals was determined by a random shuffle of four cards, two marked "cake" and two marked "banana."

Children could select a yellow or red brick from those remaining in piles or a brick already allocated to the monkey or horse. They were encouraged to put a brick on the plate by the experimenter, who said, "Go on—put some banana/cake on the plate," but no feedback was given until a brick had been so placed. If an incorrect choice was made, the experimenter said, "No, that's banana/cake," returned the brick to its earlier location, and placed a correct brick on the plate, saying, "The ——— wants some banana/cake." The animal and the correct block were then removed to one side, and the next animal was introduced.

Results

Two children (one younger child on Trials 2–4, and one older child on Trials 2–3) failed to make a response; this was recorded as an incorrect choice. All other responses involved selecting a brick from the remaining piles. No child attempted to retrieve the bricks that either the experimenter or the child had allocated to the monkey or the horse, even though these were within easy reach.

Children were scored for the number of trials (out of four) on which they made a correct choice of brick (prior to receiving feedback on a given trial). Table 4 shows the number of children in each age group who made a correct choice on zero, one, two, three, or four trials. More than half the younger children (9 out of 15) and most of the older children (13 out of

TABLE 4

EXPERIMENT 2: NUMBER OF YOUNGER (N = 15) AND OLDER
(N = 15) CHILDREN MAKING 0, 1, 2, 3,
OR 4 CORRECT CHOICES

	NUMBER OF CORRECT CHOICES					
GROUP	0	1	2	3	4	MEAN
Younger	0	3	3	4	5	2.73
Older	1	1	0	5	8	3.20

15) were correct on either three or all four trials. Two-tailed Kolmogorov-Smirnov tests showed that the distribution of subjects differed from chance for the older group, $D(N = 15) = 0.555, p < .01$, but not for the younger group, $D(N = 15) = 0.288, p < .15$.

Performance on Trial 1 was examined separately because subsequent performance might have been influenced by the experimenter's feedback. Twelve of 15 younger subjects and 14 of 15 older subjects made a correct choice on the first trial. Two-tailed binomial tests confirmed that both these results differed from chance ($p < .036$ for the younger group, $p < .005$ for the older group).

In summary, there was clear-cut evidence of appropriate choice by the older children both on Trial 1 and throughout the test phase. Most younger children made a correct choice on the initial trial, but their performance across the test period did not differ from chance. Children invariably responded to the experimenter's invitation by extrapolating to hitherto unused bricks rather than by retrieving previously allocated ones.

Discussion

Children ranging in age from 25 to 33 months demonstrated a capacity for identity extrapolation by choosing between the yellow and the red bricks depending on the experimenter's stipulation of the animal's pretend desires. The beginnings of this capacity were also seen in the initial trial among children in the 19–23-month age range; however, this group's performance on subsequent trials was less systematic.

It is important to emphasize that all children chose previously unused bricks. Thus, not only did they grasp and remember the identity of the bricks that the experimenter had named in the course of feeding the monkey and the horse, but they also applied this make-believe identity to new instances. Like the children described by Walton (1990), they accepted that a make-believe stipulation extends across time and space to apply to new instances, even if there has been no explicit agreement to that effect or naming of those instances.

It might be argued that, rather than pretending, the children were merely learning to associate unfamiliar words (i.e., "banana" and "cake") with the particular brick so named by the experimenter. However, were this so, performance on the first trial should have been low, with subsequent improvement over trials—and this was not the pattern that we observed. Moreover, studies of lexical acquisition indicate that "banana" and "cake" are within the vocabulary of most 24-month-olds (cf. Fenson et al., 1991; and Nelson, 1973). These data further strengthen the claim that our subjects, especially those in the older group, realized that the experimenter was pretending when she used these terms for the bricks.

A more subtle version of the word-learning objection is that the children may have thought that the experimenter was extending the word to a novel albeit peripheral member of the category. After all, children themselves engage in such extensions and overextensions. Ideally, the presence of "knowing smiles" or explicit statements that the brick was "not really" a banana (or cake) would counter this objection. In the absence of such evidence, we reconsider this objection in reviewing the results of Experiments 3, 4, and 6, whose findings cannot be explained in terms of extension or overextension.

Taken together, Experiments 1 and 2 show that young 2-year-olds respond appropriately to an adult's make-believe stipulation. When an adult refers to an imaginary entity, these children selectively act on props associated with that imaginary entity (Experiment 1), and, when an object is named in terms of a substitute identity, they extrapolate that substitution to new props (Experiment 2). Children younger than 2 years are more limited in their response to make-believe stipulations: they do act selectively on props, but they are less likely to produce two pretend schemas in succession; they also extrapolate, but less systematically.

III. ADJUSTING PRETEND ACTIONS TO
A MAKE-BELIEVE IDENTITY

A child who has understood an adult's make-believe stipulation should not only accept the resulting pretense identity but also produce novel pretend actions tailored to that identity. In Experiments 1 and 2, children needed only to reproduce a make-believe action that they had either seen or produced in the warm-up phase. In Experiments 3 and 4, by contrast, children were required to display their understanding of the adult's pretense initiative by engaging in a novel act of pretense.

EXPERIMENT 3

Three props were introduced in the context of a game of make-believe. The experimenter referred to each prop in terms of its make-believe identity and then invited the child to act on the prop in a way that suited that identity (e.g., use a stick to stir Teddy's tea with the "spoon").

Garvey (1984, p. 169) points out that the same prop can assume a different pretense identity depending on the make-believe context that is currently operative. For example, wooden boards might serve as beams for a play house, as skis, or as weapons for a fort. Dunn and Dale (1984) report a pretend episode where a readily available object (a cushion) was allocated two different identities during the same pretend session. This flexibility of make-believe props enabled us to include a stringent control procedure to ensure that children were not merely reproducing familiar actions associated with the prop in question. Specifically, each prop was presented in the context of two different scripts that called for distinct pretend actions.

Method

Subjects

The subjects were 12 older 1-year-olds and 12 younger 2-year-olds (for details, see Table 1 above).

Procedure and Materials

Children were tested individually in their day-care group or play group. After a brief warm-up with a different set of toys, the experimenter introduced the props used to create "breakfast" and "bedtime" scripts. The order of the two scripts was counterbalanced across subjects.

The complete set of props included a large teddy bear, a tea kettle, a cup, a frying pan with spatula, an empty tube of toothpaste, a popsicle stick, a round yellow block, and a sheet of paper (30 cm × 21 cm). The last three objects were the critical target props; that is, they were deliberately chosen because they could assume more than one pretense identity in the context of the two scripts.

Each script contained three distinct episodes. For each episode, the adult engaged in a pretend action and then asked the child to complete the theme through his or her own pretense actions. For *Episode 1* of the breakfast script, the experimenter first simulated pouring tea from a teapot into an empty cup containing a popsicle stick and then handed the cup to the child, saying, "Show me how you stir Teddy's tea with the spoon." For *Episode 2,* the experimenter placed a round yellow block in an electric frying pan, simulated turning on the pan, and then used a spatula to transfer the block to a plate, saying, "Teddy's egg is ready." The plate and a fork were then handed to the child as the experimenter said, "Teddy is hungry. Show me how you give Teddy some egg to eat." For *Episode 3*, the experimenter pointed to the teddy bear, saying, "Oh dear, Teddy's got egg all over his face." She then handed the child a sheet of paper, saying, "Show me how you wipe Teddy's face with this towel."

For *Episode 1* of the bedtime script, the experimenter pretended to squeeze toothpaste onto a popsicle stick, saying, "It's time to brush Teddy's teeth now." She then handed the popsicle stick to the child, saying, "Here's Teddy's toothbrush. Show me how you brush Teddy's teeth with the toothbrush." For *Episode 2*, the experimenter said, "Now it's time for Teddy to wash up." Then she handed the yellow block to the child, saying, "Show me how you wash Teddy with the soap." For *Episode 3*, the experimenter said, "It's time for Teddy to go to sleep now. Here's Teddy's pillow," as she placed a sheet of paper on the floor. The experimenter then said, "Show me how Teddy puts his head on the pillow and goes to sleep."

The three target props and the critical request made for each prop in the two scripts are listed in Table 5. (For comparison purposes, the props and requests used in Experiment 4 are also listed.)

Scoring and Reliability

Children's responses to all six episodes were scored as correct, incorrect, or no response. A correct response involved a pretend action that was ap-

TABLE 5

EXPERIMENTS 3 AND 4: TARGET PROP AND REQUEST
FOR THE THREE EPISODES OF EACH SCRIPT

A. EXPERIMENT 3

Breakfast Script

1. Popsicle stick	"Show me how you stir Teddy's tea with the spoon."
2. Block	"Show me how you give Teddy some egg to eat."
3. Sheet of paper	"Show me how you wipe Teddy's face with this towel."

Bedtime Script

1. Popsicle stick	"Show me how you brush Teddy's teeth with the toothbrush."
2. Block	"Show me how you wash Teddy with the soap."
3. Sheet of paper	"Show me how Teddy puts his head on the pillow and goes to sleep."

B. EXPERIMENT 4

Bedtime Script

1. Block	"Show me what Teddy does with his soap."
2. Popsicle stick	"Show me what Teddy does with his comb."
3. Sheet of paper	"Show me what Teddy does with his pillow."

Dinner Script

1. Block	"Show me what Teddy does with his sandwich."
2. Popsicle stick	"Show me what Teddy does with his spoon."
3. Sheet of paper	"Show me what Teddy does with his flannel."

propriate to the experimenter's request but did not need to involve an elaborate act of pretense; for example, a child who put the stick to the teddy bear's mouth without engaging in obvious "brushing" movements was considered to have brushed Teddy's teeth. An incorrect response was scored when the child manipulated the teddy bear or the props but did not simulate the action requested. Occasionally, subjects produced a pretend response that was inappropriate to the request made in the script; for example, in the breakfast script, the popsicle stick might be used to feed the teddy bear rather than to stir his tea. These responses were also scored as incorrect. No response was scored when the child did nothing or ignored the props altogether. Reliability was assessed by having a second person present for 25% of the sessions. Percentage agreement between the two observers (calculated as agreements divided by agreements plus disagreements) was 92%.

TABLE 6

EXPERIMENT 3: MEAN NUMBER OF CORRECT RESPONSES
BY YOUNGER ($N = 12$) AND OLDER ($N = 12$)
CHILDREN FOR EACH SCRIPT

	SCRIPT	
GROUP	Breakfast	Bedtime
Younger	1.0	1.2
	(1.0)	(1.1)
Older	2.4	2.5
	(.6)	(.6)

NOTE.—Standard deviations are given in parentheses.

Results

Failures to respond were rare (5% of responses). The majority of responses were correct. Table 6 presents the mean number of correct responses (maximum = 3) for both the breakfast and the bedtime scripts by age of the child. A 2 (age) × 2 (script) ANOVA, with repeated measures on the second factor, showed that older children produced a greater number of correct responses ($M = 2.45$) than younger children ($M = 1.10$), $F(1,22) = 25.87$, $p < .0001$. Neither the main effect of script nor the interaction of age × script reached significance, $F < 1$ in each case.

The principal aim of the data analysis was to assess children's ability to use a single object appropriately in two different pretense situations. Accordingly, we also analyzed dual responses to the three target props: the popsicle stick, yellow block, and sheet of paper. To receive credit for dual usage, the child had to employ the given prop in accordance with its make-believe identity in each of the two scripts; appropriate pretense usage in only one of the scripts received no credit. Thus, scores for dual usage could range from 0 to 3 (see Table 7).

Overall, older children demonstrated a much stronger capacity than

TABLE 7

EXPERIMENT 3: NUMBER OF YOUNGER ($N = 12$) AND
OLDER ($N = 12$) CHILDREN PRODUCING 0, 1,
2, OR 3 DUAL RESPONSES

	NUMBER OF DUAL RESPONSES				
GROUP	0	1	2	3	MEAN
Younger	7	4	1	0	.50
Older	1	2	6	3	1.92

younger children to display dual usage (M = 1.92 and 0.50, respectively). The majority of older children produced a dual response for at least two of the target props, whereas the majority of younger children either were unable to demonstrate dual usage or did so only once. A Fisher exact probability test confirmed that these two proportions differed significantly ($p <$ .005).

Discussion

Experiment 3 extended the results of Experiments 1 and 2. Not only did the older children acknowledge the make-believe stipulation implied by the adult's request, but they also produced a novel action tailored to that request. They recognized that any given prop has a flexible status allowing it to be infused with more than one make-believe identity. A stick can be a spoon or a toothbrush.

The reactions of the younger children were more equivocal. They produced fewer pretend responses than the older children as well as fewer dual responses. Nonetheless, a minority of this group produced at least one dual response.

One possible explanation for this age difference is that the older children were better able to take advantage of the linguistic "clues" embedded in the experimenter's request (see Table 5 above). For example, when the experimenter invited children to stir Teddy's tea or brush Teddy's teeth, the older group may have profited from their knowledge of the key words ("stir"/"brush") in each request. Arguably, children could produce an appropriate response by focusing on these words alone, without fully understanding the pretend script. To assess the plausibility of this explanation, linguistic "clues" were eliminated in Experiment 4.

EXPERIMENT 4

Experiment 4 was modeled on Experiment 3, with one important modification. Children were no longer given a request that specified a familiar action; instead, the experimenter used a more general prompt. This modification was intended to assess whether children could produce an appropriate pretend action in the absence of any linguistic prompting.

Method

Subjects

The subjects were 15 older 1-year-olds and 15 younger 2-year-olds (for details, see Table 1 above).

Procedure and Materials

The warm-up and testing procedures were modeled on Experiment 3. A set of everyday objects was used to create two pretense scripts: a dinner theme of feeding a teddy bear and a bedtime theme of washing a teddy bear and putting it to sleep. The order of the two scripts was counterbalanced across subjects.

The props included a large teddy bear and three critical target props—a popsicle stick in a bowl, a round yellow block, and a sheet of paper (30 cm × 21 cm)—that could assume different pretense identities in the context of the dinner and bedtime themes.

The experimenter first provided a general description of the setting for each script. Then, for each of the three episodes of the script, the experimenter (1) introduced the target prop by indicating what Teddy was doing, (2) presented the child with the prop while stating the name of the object that it stood for, and (3) asked the child to show how Teddy would use the object in question.

Thus, for the bedtime script, the experimenter began by saying, "OK. Now it's time for Teddy to go into the bathroom and get ready for bed." The experimenter then continued as follows: For *Episode 1*, "Teddy is having a bath. This is Teddy's soap [offering yellow block]. Show me what Teddy does with his soap." For *Episode 2*, "Teddy is getting ready for bed. This is Teddy's comb [offering popsicle stick in bowl]. Show me what Teddy does with his comb." For *Episode 3*, "Teddy is ready to go to bed now. This is Teddy's pillow [offering piece of paper]. Show me what Teddy does with his pillow."

For the dinner script, the experimenter began by saying, "OK. Now it's time for Teddy to go into the kitchen and have his dinner." She then continued as follows: For *Episode 1*, "Teddy is having his dinner. This is Teddy's sandwich [offering yellow block]. Show me what Teddy does with his sandwich." For *Episode 2*, "Teddy is having his pudding. This is Teddy's spoon [offering popsicle stick in bowl]. Show me what Teddy does with his spoon." For *Episode 3*, "Teddy has finished his dinner now. This is Teddy's flannel [offering piece of paper]. Show me what Teddy does with his flannel." The target props and the request for the three episodes of each script are listed in Table 5 above.

Results

As in Experiment 3, responses were allocated to three categories: correct, incorrect, and no response. Table 8 shows the mean number of correct responses (maximum = 3) for both the dinner and the bedtime scripts by age of the child. A 2 (age) × 2 (script) ANOVA, with repeated measures

TABLE 8

EXPERIMENT 4: MEAN NUMBER OF CORRECT RESPONSES
BY YOUNGER (N = 15) AND OLDER (N = 15)
CHILDREN FOR EACH SCRIPT

	SCRIPT	
GROUP	Bedtime	Dinner
Younger	.8	1.5
	(.9)	(1.0)
Older	1.5	2.4
	(1.3)	(.8)

NOTE.—Standard deviations are given in parentheses.

on the second factor, revealed that older children produced a greater number of correct responses (M = 1.97) than younger children (M = 1.17), $F(1,28)$ = 6.38, p < .018. In addition, more correct responses were produced for the dinner than for the bedtime script, $F(1,28)$ = 13.90, p < .0009. The interaction of age × script was not significant, $F(1,28)$ = 0.10, N.S.

As in Experiment 3, we analyzed children's ability to use each of the three props appropriately with each script. Scores for dual usage could range from 0 to 3. Older children demonstrated a much stronger capacity than younger children to respond appropriately to the two different pretense identities (M = 1.40 and 0.46, respectively). As seen in Table 9, just over half the older children produced a dual response for at least two of the target props, whereas almost all the younger children either were unable to demonstrate dual usage or did so only once. A Fisher exact probability test confirmed that these two proportions differed significantly (p < .01).

Discussion

As compared to children in the younger group, children in the older group produced more correct pretend responses overall as well as more dual responses. The competence of the older group was particularly convincing. Even though the adult gave no indication of the specific action to be performed on the prop, these children adjusted their pretense appropriately. Because the same prop was used with each script, the children's pretense action must have been guided by the script-dependent identity of the prop even though critical action words that might assist the child in making a pretend response were removed.

In discussing Experiment 2, we pointed out that children might have treated the adult's reference to "tea" or "cake" as an overextension of literal

TABLE 9

Experiment 4: Number of Younger ($N = 15$) and Older ($N = 15$) Children Producing 0, 1, 2, or 3 Dual Responses

	Number of Dual Responses				
Group	0	1	2	3	Mean
Younger	10	4	0	1	.46
Older	5	2	5	3	1.40

usage rather than as a nonliteral pretend usage. In principle, this objection might be applicable to the results of Experiments 3 and 4. For instance, since a popsicle stick has multiple uses in everyday life, a 2-year-old might hear it described more or less literally as a spoon, not just as a stick. However, note that, outside pretend play, children are most unlikely to have heard a popsicle stick described as a comb, or a block described as soap or a sandwich, or a piece of paper described as a pillow or a flannel. Yet 40%, 60%, and 40%, respectively, of the older group gained credit for dual usage of these three props. Thus, children may have occasionally interpreted the adult as producing a familiar overextension, but this interpretation cannot explain the prevalence of dual usage among the older children.

One other finding worth emphasizing is that most children's errors consisted of manipulating the props in a literal fashion. In both Experiment 3 and Experiment 4, 88% of the incorrect responses fell into this category. Thus, children rarely produced an incorrect response that included a pretend component that was inappropriate to the ongoing script.

The results of Experiments 3 and 4 offer a consistent picture: in both, children adjusted their pretense to the temporary identity conferred on the prop by a particular script, and, in each, the measure of dual usage showed that younger 2-year-olds did so more readily than older 1-year-olds. As we noted in Chapter I, children's spontaneous play suggests that they do produce multiple substitutions during successive episodes of pretend play (Dunn & Dale, 1984, ex. 1). However, to the best of our knowledge, this is the first demonstration that 2-year-olds can keep track of such multiple substitutions. In the final chapter, we consider how children might successfully acknowledge a given pretend identity during one pretend episode without overextending that identity into the next episode.

IV. UNDERSTANDING MAKE-BELIEVE TRANSFORMATIONS

In games of pretense, a player can not only stipulate a make-believe entity (as the adult did in Experiments 1–4) but also transform it. To respond appropriately, the partner must then take account of both the stipulation and the transformation. Experiment 5 examined children's understanding of such make-believe transformations.

EXPERIMENT 5

Experiment 5 was designed with two considerations in mind. First, it was assumed that children would understand pretend transformations in light of their familiarity with real-world transformations. Thus, they would understand that pretend liquid can be poured or that a pretend substance can be squeezed, particularly when such pretend transformations were part of familiar everyday scripts such as pouring cereal from a carton or squeezing toothpaste from a tube. Second, we recognize that make-believe play often calls for the adaptation and transformation of "real-life" routines. Indeed, it seems likely that toddlers first experience the excitement of narrative through pretend play that confronts them with an unexpected breach of an otherwise familiar routine and requires a working out of its ramifications. At a pretend tea party, for example, instead of pouring imaginary tea into a cup and then drinking it, a play partner can pour the imaginary tea over one of the guests or invert the cup and pour the tea on the floor. To appreciate such transformations, children need to grasp not only the sequence of events that ordinarily constitute a given script but also the causal links between successive, *unexpected* events. Specifically, in the example given above, they need to understand that, when the teapot is tilted or the teacup inverted, imaginary tea will pour out, whether or not a conventional receptacle is in place. Accordingly, we designed Experiment 5 to include familiar transformations embedded in unexpected causal sequences.

Method

Subjects

The subjects were 15 older 1-year-olds and 15 younger 2-year-olds (for details, see Table 1 above).

Procedure and Materials

Children were presented with four episodes all of which involved "naughty Teddy" (a hand puppet manipulated by the experimenter) and two toy pigs. At the beginning of each episode, the two pigs were first positioned within easy reach on either side of the child; the experimenter said, "Here's Teddy. He's being naughty again. Look what he's doing," as she made the hand puppet carry out the episode-specific pretend action using appropriate props. Children were then asked to respond with a pretend action involving a different prop. The request included a specification of (1) the pretend action and (2) the imaginary consequence of Teddy's naughty behavior. The particular props, action, and outcome for each of the episodes were as follows.

Episode A.—The props are a teapot and a small towel. The experimenter makes Teddy pour make-believe tea over the pig situated to the right of the child and says, "Oh dear! Can you dry the pig who's all wet?" The child is then given the towel.

Episode B.—The props are a cereal box and a brush. The experimenter makes Teddy pour make-believe cereal on the floor beside the pig to the right of the child and says, "Oh dear! Can you clean the floor where it's all dirty!" The child is then given the brush.

Episode C.—The props are a tube of toothpaste (with the top on) and a tissue. The experimenter makes Teddy squirt make-believe toothpaste onto the tail of the pig to the left of the child and says, "Oh dear! Can you clean the pig who's all dirty!" The child is then given the tissue.

Episode D.—The props are an empty carton of milk and a sponge. The experimenter makes Teddy pour make-believe milk in front of the pig to the left of the child and says, "Oh dear! Can you dry the floor where it's all wet!" The child is then given the sponge.

The order of the four episodes varied randomly across children. Across the four episodes, a correct response called equally often for an action on the pigs versus the floor, acting on the left versus the right, and drying something wet versus cleaning something dirty.

TABLE 10

EXPERIMENT 5: NUMBER OF YOUNGER (N = 15) AND OLDER
(N = 15) CHILDREN MAKING 0, 1, 2, 3,
OR 4 CORRECT RESPONSES

GROUP	NUMBER OF CORRECT RESPONSES					MEAN
	0	1	2	3	4	
Younger	6	1	1	4	3	1.80
Older	2	0	1	2	10	3.20

Results

Children's responses were categorized as correct, incorrect, and no response. Correct responses were actions of cleaning or drying directed to the
right location (i.e., the pig or floor situated on the side that had been made
"wet" or "dirty"), and incorrect ones were those directed to the wrong location (i.e., the pig or floor on the side that remained "dry" or "clean"). Although children made left-right position errors, they always acted on the
appropriate surface (floor) or object (pig). No response was recorded if
children failed to use the prop that they had been given.

Table 10 shows the number of children in each age group producing
zero, one, two, three, or four correct responses. Older children performed
very well; a clear majority produced at least three correct responses. Among
younger children, by contrast, almost half produced no more than one
correct response. A Kolmogorov-Smirnov two-tailed test confirmed that the
distribution of subjects differed from what would be expected by chance in
the older group, $D(N = 15) = 0.605$, $p < .01$, but not in the younger group,
$D(N = 15) = 0.3375$, $p < .1$.

A similar pattern emerged when responses to each episode were examined; Table 11 shows the number of correct responses by age group and
episode. The majority of older children were correct on each episode. Binomial tests (two tailed) confirmed that, for the older group, the proportion
correct was greater than chance for Episodes B ($p < .036$), C ($p < .008$),

TABLE 11

EXPERIMENT 5: NUMBER OF YOUNGER (N = 15) AND
OLDER (N = 15) CHILDREN PRODUCING A
CORRECT RESPONSE BY EPISODE

GROUP	EPISODE			
	A	B	C	D
Younger	6	6	9	6
Older	11	12	13	12

and D ($p < .036$). By contrast, the proportion correct in the younger group did not differ from chance for any of the four episodes.

Nevertheless, some of the younger children did show evidence of genuine understanding. Six among them made no response on any of the four episodes, but, of the remaining nine children, seven made only correct responses, and two made more correct than incorrect responses. Thus, all nine younger children who did respond were predominantly correct ($p < .004$, two-tailed binomial test).

Discussion

The results of Experiment 5 demonstrated that young children have a striking ability to understand pretend transformations. The great majority of older children understood that the outcome to which the experimenter referred was make-believe and directed their pretend remedial action to the appropriate location. The performance of the younger group was more equivocal, but a number of them did show a clear ability to understand nonliteral, causal transformations.

Note that children's pretend responses were not simply the product of a well-rehearsed script since the episodes were deliberately created to deviate from standard expectations. In fact, Episode C (squirting toothpaste on the pig's tail), which might be regarded as the most deviant of the four, elicited the greatest number of correct responses in each age group.

Experiments 1–5 showed that children can understand an adult's nonliteral references to a pretend substance or outcome. In Experiment 6, we examined whether children can also produce such nonliteral descriptions.

V. DESCRIBING MAKE-BELIEVE TRANSFORMATIONS

In Experiment 5, children occasionally commented on the make-believe transformations by noting that one of the animals was "wet" or "dirty." Such remarks may have reflected an understanding of the pretense, or they may have echoed the experimenter's words. Hence, Experiments 6 and 7 were undertaken to explore children's ability to describe pretend transformations more systematically. These experiments had two main goals. First, if children can watch a pretend transformation and describe what has taken place appropriately, such additional evidence of their understanding would consolidate the claims made in the previous chapter. Second, children's ability to describe pretend episodes is an important psycholinguistic phenomenon in its own right. In Experiment 5, children watched while a make-believe substance was subjected to an incongruous displacement (e.g., poured over a pig): a full description of this event would have to involve a reference to the make-believe substance (tea) and the make-believe outcome (the pig is wet). Thus, the child must use language nonliterally to refer to an entity and an outcome that do not actually exist. Experiment 6 was designed to assess whether children can provide such nonliteral descriptions. In order to reduce the potential interpretive problems posed by the limited vocabulary of children younger than 2 years, we tested children ranging in age from 24 to 36 months. The mean age of the younger group was 28 months (i.e., comparable to the older group of Experiments 1–5), and the mean age of the older group was 34 months.

EXPERIMENT 6

Method

Subjects

Subjects were 16 younger 2-year-olds and 16 older 2-year-olds (for details, see Table 1 above). Two further children were tested but not included in the final sample: one child (aged 25 months) was very shy and made no verbal response on any episode; the other child (aged 31 months) was excluded to equate numbers in the two age groups.

Procedure

The experimenter began by introducing the "naughty Teddy" hand puppet, with whom she then acted out four episodes. Having completed the episode-specific action (e.g., in Episode A, Teddy was made to pour pretend tea over the monkey's head), the experimenter asked the child four questions. Question 1 was open ended; subsequent questions focused more explicitly on the imaginary substance used by Teddy (Question 2) and on the outcome for the target of his action (Questions 3 and 4). Thus, for Episode A, the questions were as follows:

1. "What happened—what did Teddy do?"
2. "What did Teddy put on the monkey's head?"
3. "Teddy did this, didn't he?" [said as the experimenter made Teddy briefly repeat his action]. "Teddy made the monkey's head all . . . ?"
4. "Is the monkey's head wet or dry?"

The procedure for the other three episodes was similar. Teddy's pretend action in each episode, the imaginary substance, the target of Teddy's action, and the outcome for the toy animal are listed in Table 12. In the subsequent set of four questions, Question 1 remained constant across the four episodes, Questions 2–4 mentioned the appropriate target of Teddy's action, and Question 4 mentioned the pretend outcome and its semantic opposite in an order counterbalanced across the four episodes. The order of the four episodes was randomly varied across children. Children's verbal replies were tape-recorded for later transcription. Owing to experimenter error, three children (one younger child and two older) were not asked Question 4.

TABLE 12

EXPERIMENT 6: ACTION, IMAGINARY SUBSTANCE, CONTAINER, TARGET, AND OUTCOME IN FOUR PRETEND EPISODES

Episode	Action	Substance	Container	Target	Outcome
A	Poured	Tea	Teapot	Monkey's head	Wet/dry
B	Squirted	Toothpaste	Tube	Rabbit's ear	Dirty/clean
C	Poured	Milk	Carton	Horse's tail	Wet/dry
D	Brushed	Paint	Palette	Pig's nose	Dirty/clean

Results

Children were surprisingly articulate in responding to the experimenter's questions. In reply to the initial open-ended question, they referred to Teddy's pretend action, the imaginary substance involved, and its direction. Although they rarely mentioned the outcome in their initial reply, they often did so in response to Questions 3 and 4. Replies to each of the four questions are analyzed in turn.

Question 1

Replies to Question 1 were examined for references to nonliteral aspects of the episode. No credit was given for references to the container that Teddy had used or the toy animal that he had victimized since such references would be included in a literal description. Credit was awarded only when the child referred appropriately to Teddy's pretend *action* (e.g., "poured"), the imaginary *substance* (e.g., "tea"), its implied *direction* (e.g., "onto"), and the implied *outcome* (e.g., "wet"). This scoring scheme proved applicable to all four episodes. Table 13 lists the words or phrases considered appropriate for each episode and category (i.e., *action, substance, direction,* and *outcome*).

The child was credited with one point for giving an appropriate nonliteral reply in the given category. Since preliminary inspection of the data showed that scores were stable across episodes, these were summed across episodes, yielding a maximum score of four points for each category and of 16 points across categories. Table 14 shows mean correct scores by age and category. Children often mentioned the pretend action, substance, and direction, especially in the older age group, but spontaneous references to outcomes were rare at both ages. A mixed 2 (age) × 4 (category) ANOVA revealed main effects for age, $F(1,30) = 11.016$, $p < .01$, and category,

TABLE 13

EXPERIMENT 6: RESPONSES JUDGED CORRECT BY CATEGORY AND EPISODE, QUESTION 1

	RESPONSE CATEGORY			
EPISODE	Action	Substance	Direction	Outcome
A	"tipped"/"poured"/"put"	"tea"	"on"/"over"	"wet"
B	"put"/"squeezed"	"toothpaste"	"on"/"over"	[a]
C	"put"/"poured"	"milk"	"on"	"wet"
D	"drawing"/"painted"/"put"/ "brushed"	"paint"	"on"/"over"	[a]

[a] No child produced a response that received credit.

TABLE 14

Experiment 6: Mean Number of Nonliteral Responses (out of
4) by Younger (N = 16) and Older (N = 16) Children for
Each Response Category, Question 1

	RESPONSE CATEGORY			
GROUP	Action	Substance	Direction	Outcome
Younger	1.4	1.3	1.2	.2
	(1.6)	(1.1)	(1.2)	(.4)
Older	2.6	2.8	2.5	.1
	(1.1)	(1.0)	(1.1)	(.2)

Note.—Standard deviations are given in parentheses.

$F(3,90) = 37.217$, $p < .001$, as well as an age × category, $F(3,90) = 5.855$, $p < .01$, interaction.

Further analysis of this interaction confirmed that both age groups were equally unlikely to mention the outcome of Teddy's transgressions, $F(1,60) = 0.125$, N.S., but older children were more likely than younger children to refer to the pretend action, $F(1,60) = 4.174$, $p < .05$, the imaginary substance, $F(1,60) = 7.420$, $p < .01$, and its implied direction, $F(1,60) = 5.681$, $p < .05$.

Question 2

In Question 2, children were asked what imaginary substance Teddy had displaced. Acceptable replies for Episodes A, B, C, and D were, respectively, "tea," "toothpaste," "milk," and "paint." Responses were again stable across the four episodes. Accordingly, children were scored in terms of the number of episodes (out of four) for which they received credit. Table 15 shows the number of children in each age group who received credit for zero, one, two, three, or four episodes and the group mean score. Most children in both age groups gave appropriate replies in at least three episodes. Although the mean score was somewhat higher for the older chil-

TABLE 15

Experiment 6: Number of Younger (N = 16) and Older
(N = 16) Children Receiving Credit on 0–4
Episodes, Question 2

	NUMBER OF CORRECT RESPONSES					
GROUP	0	1	2	3	4	MEAN
Younger	1	2	1	4	8	3.00
Older	1	1	0	5	9	3.25

TABLE 16

EXPERIMENT 6: ACCEPTABLE RESPONSES BY EPISODE AND TYPE OF RESPONSE, QUESTION 3

	CATEGORY OF RESPONSE		
EPISODE	Conventional Adjectives	Unconventional Adjectives	Substantives
A	"dirty"/"black"/"wet"/"soggy"/"grubby"	"soaky"/"teay"	"tea"
B	"mucky"/"pink"/"messy"/"wet"/"grubby"/ "toothy"/"covered"	"toothpastey"	"toothpaste"
C	"wet"/"milky"/"dirty"/"soggy"/"grubby"	. . .	"milk"
D	"dirty"/"pink"/"wet"/"red"	"painty"	"paint"

dren, a Kolmogorov-Smirnov (two-tailed) test revealed no significant difference between the two age groups, $D(N = 16) = 2$, N.S.

Question 3

In Question 3, children were prompted to say what happened to Teddy's victim. Most replies fell into one of three categories shown in Table 16: conventional adjectives (e.g., "wet," "soggy," "dirty," "milky"), invented adjectives (e.g., "soaky," "teay," "toothpastey," "painty"), and, finally, references to the appropriate substance with no adjectival suffix (e.g., "tea," "toothpaste," "paint").

Replies in this last category are ambiguous. Children may have been simply echoing their reply to Question 2 (which required them to identify the imaginary substance), or they may have been using the substantive as an adjective. Note that these substantives are legitimately used as adjectives by adults (e.g., "teacup," "milk chocolate," "paint job"). Given the plausibility of either interpretation, these replies were coded in two different ways. Under a strict scoring system, children received credit for producing conventional or unconventional adjectives, but substantives were not given credit. Under the liberal scoring system, they were credited for producing either type of adjective as well as for an appropriate substantive. Table 17 shows the number of children in each age group who received credit for zero to four episodes under each scoring system.

Both age groups responded similarly. Under the conservative scoring system, the majority of both younger and older children received credit for at least one episode; with liberal scoring, they received credit for at least three episodes. Kolmogorov-Smirnov (two-tailed) tests confirmed that the two age groups did not differ using either scoring system (conservative, $D[N = 16] = 6$, N.S.; liberal, $D[N = 16] = 4$, N.S.).

Children's replies were examined further to assess their independence

TABLE 17

Experiment 6: Number of Younger ($N = 16$) and Older
($N = 16$) Children Receiving Credit on 0–4 Episodes
Using Conservative and Liberal Scoring, Question 3

Scoring and Group	Number of Correct Responses					Mean
	0	1	2	3	4	
Conservative:						
Younger	4	7	2	2	1	1.31
Older	2	3	4	6	1	2.06
Liberal:						
Younger	2	2	2	3	7	2.69
Older	0	1	3	1	11	3.38

from the adjectives used by the experimenter. Replies credited under conservative scoring were divided into three types: *repetitions,* or words that the experimenter had used during a previous episode (e.g., "wet," "dirty"); (2) *independent but conventional adjectives,* or standard adjectives that the experimenter had never used (e.g., "soggy," "grubby") as well as adjectives eventually used by the experimenter but produced first by the child; and (3) *unconventional adjectives* (e.g., "painty," "toothpastey"). Table 18 shows the number of younger and older children who produced each type of reply.

The data show that children did not confine their descriptions of the imagined outcome to repetitions of the experimenter's words but rather used other adjectives, including those of their own invention. In total, eight

TABLE 18

Experiment 6: Number of Younger ($N = 16$) and Older
($N = 16$) Children Producing the Different Types
of Replies for 0–4 Episodes, Question 3

Scoring and Group	Number of Correct Responses					Mean
	0	1	2	3	4	
Repetitions:						
Younger	9	6	0	1	0	.56
Older	10	4	1	1	0	.56
Independent:						
Younger	10	4	2	0	0	.50
Older	5	6	3	2	0	1.13
Unconventional:						
Younger	0	4	0	0	0	.25
Older	0	2	2	0	0	.38

younger children and 12 older children produced at least one reply falling into the independent or the unconventional category.

Question 4

In Question 4, children were offered a forced choice of descriptors for the pretend outcome of "naughty Teddy's" actions. As shown in Table 19, the majority of children in each age group made the correct choice in all four episodes. Kolmogorov-Smirnov (two-tailed) tests confirmed that the distribution of subjects differed from chance for both younger, $D(N = 15) = 0.605, p < .01$, and older, $D(N = 14) = 0.652, p < .01$, subjects. The proportion of subjects who were correct in all four episodes did not differ between the two age groups (by Fisher exact probability test).

Discussion

The results of Experiment 6 show that 2-year-olds are able to describe a make-believe transformation. In response to the initial open-ended question, children mentioned the pretend action, the pretend substance, and the direction of its displacement, but references to the implied outcome were rare. This pattern of responding was observed in both age groups, although it was more systematic in the older group.

In response to the follow-up questions, the majority of children in each age group correctly identified the imaginary substance in at least three episodes. They were able to describe the pretend outcome with varying degrees of inventiveness: some reiterated an adjective previously used by the experimenter, others used their own conventional and appropriate adjectives, and a minority invented their own nonconventional adjectives. Finally, when asked to choose between two opposing descriptions of the outcome, the great majority of children in both age groups responded correctly.

These findings warrant two conclusions. First, they confirm the results

TABLE 19

EXPERIMENT 6: NUMBER OF YOUNGER AND OLDER CHILDREN
MAKING CORRECT REPLIES FOR 0–4 EPISODES, QUESTION 4

	NUMBER OF CORRECT REPLIES						
GROUP	0	1	2	3	4	N^a	MEAN
Younger	0	1	3	1	10	15	3.33
Older	0	1	1	2	10	14	3.50

[a] One younger and two older children were not asked Question 4, reducing the N for each age group.

of Experiment 5: 2-year-olds can readily comprehend a make-believe trans-formation. By following the movements of an associated prop, such as a container or a receptacle, they are able to work out that an imaginary sub-stance has been displaced. They also correctly infer the consequences for the target of the pretend action; that is, they realize that the victim becomes "wet" or "dirty" even though no such perceptual change is evident.

Second, these results show that 2-year-olds can translate what they have understood about make-believe transformations into words. Children of-fered such descriptions with surprising facility, identifying the imaginary substance and the implied outcome even though, as noted above, neither could actually be observed.

Children's descriptions of the implied outcome bear on the previously noted possibility that they may have perceived the adult's use of the words "banana," "cake," and "spoon" in Experiments 2–4 as an extension to pe-ripheral instances of those categories, not as a genuinely nonliteral usage. Children's description of the outcome of Teddy's intervention cannot be interpreted in this conservative fashion. Had children interpreted Question 4 literally, they would have answered incorrectly: the monkey was literally dry, not wet, after Teddy's pretend dousing with the teapot. Thus, to reply correctly to Question 4, children must have understood the adult's reference nonliterally and replied nonliterally.

These findings have implications for the standard conception of chil-dren's linguistic development in which early language is often described as tied to the here and now. For example, Givon (1979) argues that the initial phase of language development is "overwhelmingly about the here-and-now, you-and-I, and visible objects in the immediate perceptual field" (p. 291). Brown and Bellugi (1964/1970) follow a quotation from Adam, aged 27 months, with the comment that "there is no speech of the sort that Bloomfield called 'displaced' speech about other times and places" (pp. 79–80). Subsequent research by Sachs (1983) has shown that 2-year-olds pro-duce utterances that are temporally or spatially "displaced" from current reality, but there has been little study of children's ability to engage in speech about a pretend reality.

The results of Experiment 6 show that 2-year-olds can describe what is happening in a fictitious world. "Naughty Teddy" did not actually make the monkey wet or the pig dirty; both episodes took place in the make-believe world. In Chapter VII, we attempt a fuller explanation for the constructive process that occurs when children keep track of a make-believe episode and eventually describe it.

The results also highlight another psycholinguistic phenomenon. In describing the implied outcome, a minority of children (25% in each age group) resorted at least once to their own invented but appropriate adjec-tives. These children appear to have adopted a generative rule of adding

"-(e)y" to a substantive to create a new adjectival form. The early lexicon probably contains many words that might prompt such a rule: "dirt(y)," "milk(y)," "salt(y)," and so forth. Clark (1983, p. 827) suggests that coinages that require the addition of a suffix appear after age 2 years, and our results confirm that 2-year-olds do produce such coinages.

EXPERIMENT 7

Experiment 6 showed that 2-year-olds can follow and describe a pretend transformation involving imaginary substances. The goal of Experiment 7 was to extend these findings to include substitute objects as well as imaginary substances. Accordingly, the format of the previous experiment was suitably modified.

Method

Subjects

Subjects were 11 younger 2-year-olds and 11 older 2-year-olds (for details, see Table 1 above). Two additional children were tested but not included in the final sample: one child (aged 26 months) made no verbal response to any episode; the other child (aged 31 months) replied only to the final question of Episode D and was otherwise silent.

Procedure

The experimenter began by introducing the "naughty Teddy" hand puppet, with whom she then acted out four episodes. Each episode began with the introduction of an additional toy animal and the stipulation of a prop as a pretend food. For example, in Episode A, the experimenter introduced the monkey, saying, "The monkey likes to eat chocolate. Let's give him some chocolate." A brown block was placed on a paper plate and put in front of the monkey. Then the experimenter drew the child's attention to the impending intervention: "Oh dear! Watch what naughty Teddy does," spoken as she made Teddy "pour" pretend tea from an empty teapot over the "chocolate." She then asked the child five questions:

    1. "What happened—what did Teddy do?"
    2. "What did Teddy pour?"
    3. "Where did Teddy put it?" [If children simply pointed, they were given the further prompt:] "What's that?"

4. "Teddy did this, didn't he?" [said as the experimenter made Teddy briefly repeat his action]. "Teddy made the chocolate all . . . ?"
5. "Is the chocolate wet or dry?"

The animal partner, Teddy's pretend action, the imaginary substance, and the substitute food used in each episode are listed in Table 20. The questions following each episode were adjusted depending on what Teddy had done. Thus, while Question 1 remained constant across the four episodes, Question 2 referred to either "pour" or "squeeze," Questions 4 and 5 referred to the relevant substitute food, and Question 5 referred to either "wet/dry" or "dirty/clean," with the order of the two alternatives counterbalanced across the four episodes. The order of the four episodes was randomly varied across children. Children's verbal replies were tape-recorded for later transcription.

Results

Children were again articulate in describing Teddy's transgression. They sometimes referred to the substitute food in reply to Question 1, and they did so quite systematically in reply to Question 3. This pattern of responding was stable across episodes; the sole exception was a difficulty in naming the imaginary substance in Episode D (i.e., liquid for washing dishes). However, since this difficulty characterized both age groups and did not disrupt the overall pattern of responding, the data were again summed across categories and episodes where appropriate.

Question 1

Replies to Question 1 were analyzed for references to nonliteral aspects of the episode. No credit was given for references to the container that Teddy had used because even a literal description would include such refer-

TABLE 20

EXPERIMENT 7: ACTION, IMAGINARY SUBSTANCE, CONTAINER, FOOD (Prop),
AND OUTCOME IN FOUR PRETEND EPISODES

Episode	Action	Substance	Container	Food (Prop)	Outcome[a]
A	Poured	Tea	Teapot	Chocolate (block)	Wet/dry
B	Squeezed	Toothpaste	Tube	Banana (block)	Dirty/clean
C	Poured	Milk	Carton	Sausage (Play-Doh)	Wet/dry
D	Squeezed	Liquid	Bottle	Ice cream (block)	Dirty/clean

[a] The first entry gives the outcome and the second the opposite outcome included in the forced-choice Question 5.

TABLE 21

EXPERIMENT 7: RESPONSES JUDGED CORRECT BY CATEGORY AND EPISODE, QUESTION 1

EPISODE	Action	Substance	Direction	Food
		CATEGORY		
A	"put"/"poured"	"tea"/"coffee"	"on"/"out"/"over"	"chocolate"
B	"put"/"squeezed"	"toothpaste"	"on"	"banana"
C	"put"/"poured"	"milk"	"on"	"sausage"
D	"put"/"poured"/ "spilled"	"bubbles"/"cream"/ "liquid"/"glue"/ "washing stuff"/ "ointment"	"on"/"over"	"ice cream"

ences. Credit was awarded only when children referred appropriately to Teddy's pretend *action* (e.g., "poured"), the imaginary *substance* (e.g., "tea"), its implied *direction* (e.g., "onto"), and the *substitute* (e.g., "chocolate"). This scoring scheme proved applicable to all four episodes. Table 21 lists the words or phrases that were given credit for each episode and category (i.e., *action, substance, direction,* and *substitute*). Note that the *outcome* (e.g., "wet," "dirty") was not included in the coding scheme for this question because only two children (aged 30 and 32 months) spontaneously referred to the outcome, one for Episode C ("made it dirty") and one for Episode D ("made it all messy").

Children were credited with one point for an appropriate nonliteral reply for a given category. Summed across the four episodes, children could obtain a maximum of four points for each category and 16 points across all four categories. Table 22 shows mean correct scores by age and category. Children usually mentioned the pretend action, substance, and direction for one or more episodes; the substitute food, however, was mentioned less often. A mixed 2 (age) × 2 (category) ANOVA confirmed this effect of

TABLE 22

EXPERIMENT 7: MEAN NUMBER OF NONLITERAL RESPONSES (out of 4) BY YOUNGER ($N = 11$) AND OLDER ($N = 11$) CHILDREN FOR EACH CATEGORY, QUESTION 1

GROUP	Action	Substance	Direction	Substitute
		CATEGORY		
Younger	2.3	2.0	2.3	.8
	(1.3)	(1.1)	(1.1)	(.8)
Older	3.5	2.5	3.3	2.1
	(.8)	(.9)	(.7)	(1.4)

NOTE.—Standard deviations are given in parentheses.

TABLE 23

Experiment 7: Number of Younger ($N = 11$) and Older
($N = 11$) Children Receiving Credit on 0–4
Episodes, Question 2

GROUP	NUMBER OF CORRECT RESPONSES					MEAN
	0	1	2	3	4	
Younger	1	1	0	6	3	2.82
Older	0	1	2	5	3	2.91

category, $F(3,60) = 12.200$, $p < .001$. The main effect of age also reached significance, $F(1,20) = 8.54$, $p < .01$.

Question 2

In Question 2, children were explicitly asked what imaginary substance Teddy had displaced. Acceptable replies for Episodes A–D were, respectively, "tea"/"coffee," "toothpaste"/"medicine," "milk," and "liquid"/"bubbles"/"glue"/"cream"/"washing stuff"/"ointment." As noted above, children had difficulty identifying the imaginary substance in Episode D, presumably because the container (of dishwashing liquid) was less familiar. Faced with this unfamiliarity, they produced a range of answers.

Table 23 shows the number of children in each age group who received credit for zero, one, two, three, or four episodes and the group means. Most children in both age groups gave appropriate replies for at least three episodes. The mean score was slightly higher in the older group, but a Kolmogorov-Smirnov (two-tailed) test revealed no significant difference between the two ages, $D(N = 11) = 1$, N.S.

Question 3

Credit was given for identifying the substitute food correctly (i.e., "chocolate," "banana," "sausage," and "[ice] cream"). Table 24 shows that most children in both age groups gave appropriate replies for two or more episodes. A Kolmogorov-Smirnov (two-tailed) test showed that the two age groups did not differ, $D(N = 11) = 1$, N.S.

In failing to gain credit, children typically said nothing or simply pointed to the target without naming it. However, two children gave literal replies. One (aged 28 months) said, "There—on the brick," for Episode B even though in reply to Question 1 for the same episode she had said,

TABLE 24

EXPERIMENT 7: NUMBER OF YOUNGER ($N = 11$) AND OLDER
($N = 11$) CHILDREN RECEIVING CREDIT ON 0–4
EPISODES, QUESTION 3

	NUMBER OF CORRECT RESPONSES					
GROUP	0	1	2	3	4	MEAN
Younger	1	1	2	2	5	2.81
Older	1	2	2	2	4	2.54

"Put some toothpaste on the nana." The other child (aged 31 months) said, "There, on a brick" (with minor variations), for Episodes A, B, and D.

Question 4

In Question 4, children were prompted to say what happened to the toy animal's food. Most replies fell into one of the two types shown in Table 25: conventional adjectives (e.g., "wet," "dirty," "milky") and mention of the appropriate substance with no adjectival suffix (e.g., "tea," "toothpaste"). No child coined an adjective in this experiment.

As noted previously (Experiment 6), in referring to the substance with no adjectival suffix, children may have been either simply echoing their reply to Question 2 or using the substantive as an adjective. Accordingly, replies were again coded conservatively, with credit for conventional adjectives but not substantives, as well as liberally, with credit for either type of reply. Table 26 shows the number of children in each age group who received credit for zero, one, two, three, or four episodes under each scoring system.

A clear majority of children in each age group received credit for at

TABLE 25

EXPERIMENT 7: RESPONSES JUDGED CORRECT FOR
EACH EPISODE, QUESTION 4

	TYPE OF RESPONSE	
EPISODE	Conventional Adjectives	Substantives
A	"wet"/"dirty"	"tea"
B	"wet"/"dirty"/"sticky"	"toothpaste"
C	"wet"/"dirty"/"milky"	"milk"
D	"wet"/"dirty"/"messy"	"ointment"

TABLE 26

EXPERIMENT 7: NUMBER OF YOUNGER (N = 11) AND OLDER
(N = 11) CHILDREN RECEIVING CREDIT ON 0–4 EPISODES USING
CONSERVATIVE AND LIBERAL SCORING, QUESTION 4

SCORING AND GROUP	NUMBER OF CORRECT RESPONSES					MEAN
	0	1	2	3	4	
Conservative:						
Younger	3	1	6	1	0	1.45
Older	0	3	1	2	5	2.82
Liberal:						
Younger	2	1	4	3	1	2.00
Older	0	2	1	2	6	3.09

least two episodes under either scoring system. Two Kolmogorov-Smirnov
(two-tailed) tests confirmed that the age groups did not differ (conservative,
$D[N = 11] = 6$, N.S.; liberal, $D[N = 11] = 5$, N.S.).

Children's replies were also examined to assess their independence
from adjectives used by the experimenter. Replies credited under conservative scoring were consequently divided into *repetitions,* or words that the
experimenter had used during a previous episode, and *independent but conventional adjectives,* or standard adjectives that the experimenter never used
(e.g., "soggy," "grubby") as well as adjectives eventually used by the experimenter (i.e., "wet," "dirty") but produced first by the child. Table 27 shows
the number of younger and older children who produced replies in each
of these two types.

Table 27 shows that children did not limit their descriptions of the
outcome to repetitions of the experimenter's words but also used other

TABLE 27

EXPERIMENT 7: NUMBER OF YOUNGER (N = 11) AND OLDER
(N = 11) CHILDREN PRODUCING DIFFERENT TYPES OF
REPLY FOR 0–4 EPISODES, QUESTION 4

TYPE OF REPLY AND GROUP	NUMBER OF CORRECT RESPONSES					MEAN
	0	1	2	3	4	
Repetitions:						
Younger	5	3	2	0	0	.82
Older	2	4	2	3	0	1.55
Independent:						
Younger	5	5	1	0	0	.64
Older	2	5	4	0	0	1.18

adjectives. In total, six younger and nine older children produced at least one reply of the independent type.

Question 5

In Question 5, children were offered a forced choice to describe the pretend outcome of Teddy's actions. As shown in Table 28, the majority of children in each age group were systematically correct for at least three episodes. Kolmogorov-Smirnov (two-tailed) tests showed that the distribution of subjects did not differ from chance for younger children, $D(N = 11) = 0.238$, N.S., but did differ from chance for older children, $D(N = 11) = 0.664$, $p < .01$. Nevertheless, a Kolmogorov-Smirnov (two-tailed) test revealed no difference between the two age groups, $D(N = 11) = 6$, N.S.

Discussion

Children responded to the initial open-ended question by referring to Teddy's pretend action, the substance he had poured or squeezed, and the direction of its displacement. Spontaneous references to the target of his transgression—the substitute food—were less frequent. Nevertheless, children clearly understood that Teddy had acted on the food since, when they were explicitly asked about it (Question 3), most children in each age group named it appropriately for at least two episodes. Literal descriptions of the target object (e.g., as a "brick") were very rare. Children also understood and replied appropriately to the experimenter's nonliteral questions about the outcome for the substitute food. In reply to Question 4, the majority of children in each age group described the outcome appropriately (using conservative scoring) for at least two episodes; the majority also produced an appropriate description for at least one episode before the experimenter had used the term.

These findings confirm the results of Experiment 6: children can track

TABLE 28

EXPERIMENT 7: NUMBER OF YOUNGER ($N = 11$) AND OLDER
($N = 11$) CHILDREN RECEIVING CREDIT FOR 0–4
EPISODES, QUESTION 5

	NUMBER OF CORRECT RESPONSES					
GROUP	0	1	2	3	4	MEAN
Younger	0	2	3	4	2	2.55
Older	0	1	1	1	8	3.45

a pretend transformation such as pouring or squeezing and then describe this imaginary event. The results also show that children can coordinate the successive parts of a pretend episode. In each episode, the child had to hold in mind the experimenter's initial stipulation of the make-believe identity of the brick or Play-Doh in interpreting the effect of Teddy's pretend action. Children typically did this for at least two of the episodes they watched. As we argue in the next chapter, this integration of successive components is also crucial for narrative and discourse comprehension.

In this chapter, we review several results that emerged consistently in the preceding experiments; we compare them to earlier findings and highlight some less obvious implications that must be addressed by any theoretical model.

REVIEW OF RESULTS

Experiments 1 and 2 assessed children's understanding of an adult's make-believe stipulation. A stipulation can imply either that a prop contains a make-believe entity (Experiment 1) or that a prop of a given type stands for a make-believe entity (Experiment 2). The results showed that 18–30-month-olds grasp the significance of such remarks: they chose between props in accordance with the make-believe status conferred on them. Selectivity was systematic among young 2-year-olds, but it was less systematic among children younger than 2 years.

Experiments 3 and 4 required children to respect such make-believe stipulations by acting on the prop in a novel but appropriate way. Young 2-year-olds proved very competent at acting differently toward the same prop depending on its temporary, script-based identity. Children younger than 2 years also directed correct pretend actions at the props, but they produced two different actions for the same prop less often.

Experiment 5 examined children's understanding of pretend transformations. Young 2-year-olds were able to understand the make-believe effect of pretend actions such as pouring or squeezing even when those transformations led to unfamiliar outcomes. They appropriately "dried" or "cleaned" the unexpected locations that had been made "wet" or "dirty." Many of the children younger than 2 years failed to respond at all, perhaps because they attempted to interpret the adult's request literally and could reach no plausible interpretation. However, among those younger children who did respond (60%), correct responses predominated.

Experiments 6 and 7 asked whether 2-year-olds can put their understanding of pretend transformations into words. In both experiments, children did not describe what had literally happened; instead, they referred appropriately to Teddy's pretend action, the imaginary substance he had acted on, and its implied direction. They could also infer and describe the outcome of Teddy's transgression when explicitly asked about it. Finally, in Experiment 7, children realized that Teddy's action had been directed at a substitute object; they referred to it in terms of its previously stipulated make-believe identity, not its literal identity.

Young 2-year-olds displayed considerable competence throughout this series of experiments. They understood make-believe stipulations, they produced actions tailored to the currently stipulated identity of a prop, they acted appropriately following unexpected pretend transformations, and they could talk about such pretend transformations.

The understanding of children younger than 2 years (average age = 20–22 months) was more fragile. Although these children did show some understanding of a make-believe stipulation, they were less systematic in extrapolating that stipulation to other props, in producing suitable pretend actions, and in responding appropriately to transformations.

COMPARISON WITH PREVIOUS RESEARCH

In Chapter I, we reviewed earlier research suggesting that young children can understand and respond appropriately to make-believe stipulations and transformations. Most of the studies that we reviewed were not explicitly designed to study comprehension. Rather, they were intended to show that children engaged in joint play benefit from the availability of a play partner or reproduce pretend actions previously modeled by an adult. For that reason, our conclusions with respect to comprehension were tentative. The results of Experiments 1–7 permit firmer conclusions.

The Comprehension of Make-Believe Stipulations

Dunn and Dale (1984) describe selected episodes of collaborative pretend play in which 2-year-olds appear to understand a stipulation introduced by an older sibling. Thus, 2-year-old Richard supplied make-believe "petrol" in response to his sibling's request. However, it was difficult to assess from Dunn and Dale's observational study whether such understanding is widespread among 2-year-olds. The results of Experiments 1 and 2 confirm that such comprehension is quite extensive by 28 months and can be observed in a more fragile form among children younger than 2 years.

Our results show that children understand two of the main types of stipulation identified in research on pretense production: the stipulation of make-believe entities, especially in the context of an appropriate prop such as a container (Experiment 1), and the stipulation of a make-believe substitution, especially when the substitute has no salient countervailing identity (Experiment 2).

Producing Appropriate Pretend Actions

When children watch an adult act out a pretend episode, they often subsequently reproduce what the adult has done, suggesting that they have understood the adult's make-believe stipulations (Bretherton et al., 1984; Fenson, 1984). However, the effect of modeling in such experiments is not easy to interpret. Motor imitation or literal comprehension might explain the child's reproduction.

In Experiments 3 and 4, children could not gain credit for reproduction of an adult model. They were required to produce an action appropriate to the adult's make-believe stipulation, but they had not seen the adult produce that action. The success of 2-year-olds in these two experiments shows that they understand an adult's make-believe stipulation (extending the results of Experiments 1 and 2) and that they can generate an action appropriate to that stipulation with no assistance from a model. Experiment 4 is particularly convincing in this respect because the experimenter simply conferred an identity on the ambiguous prop (appropriate to the ongoing script) without giving children clues about what pretend action they should perform with the prop.

Given the design of Experiments 3 and 4 (i.e., the use of an ambiguous prop embedded in two different pretend episodes), children could not have been prompted by the prop itself in generating an appropriate pretend action. The clear implication is that they were guided by the temporary identity conferred on the prop.

Understanding Pretend Transformations

Children's understanding of pretend transformations was studied by Leslie (1988a), who reported that 2-year-olds keep track of pretend transformations because, after watching such transformations, they join in with an appropriate comment or action. For example, they refill a container whose pretend contents have been emptied, or they describe an animal covered in pretend liquid as "wet." However, Leslie gave no quantitative analysis of his findings, and other reports (e.g., DeLoache & Plaetzer, 1985) suggest that children may respond inappropriately after a pretend transformation.

Experiments 5–7 confirm and extend Leslie's (1988a) positive results. Children watched a variety of pretend physical transformations (e.g., "pouring," "squeezing," "painting"), and these transformations led to a variety of outcomes (e.g., the target was covered in tea, toothpaste, or paint). Two-year-olds demonstrated comprehension of these changes by their appropriate remedial action in Experiment 5 and their appropriate descriptions in Experiments 6 and 7.

The Use of Pretend Language

Few previous studies of pretend play have systematically examined the production of pretend language. Ungerer, Zelazo, Kearsley, and O'Leary (1981) reported that appropriate pretend references to imaginary or substitute objects were quite widespread among 2-year-olds. However, it is unclear from their results whether this occurred only after modeling by an adult. Subsequent research is more informative. Fenson (1984) observed that, prior to any modeling, more than half of a group of 26-month-olds referred to the substitute identity of a prop or attributed pretend actions and states to dolls. Bretherton et al. (1984) obtained similar results. References to a pretend action, substance, state, or location were infrequent at 20 months but much more frequent at 28 months, even before any adult modeling. Moreover, after adult modeling, children used words for make-believe entities that had not been modeled.

In line with these results, we found that 2-year-olds could make appropriate reference to imaginary or substitute objects. In addition, we found that they produced (Experiments 6 and 7) and understood (Experiment 5) references to outcomes that had been created by a pretend transformation (e.g., "wet," "messy"). Thus, language is not used simply to stipulate a pretend state or identity when it is first introduced; it is also used to describe outcomes that ensue in the course of the pretend episode. As we elaborate more fully in the next chapter, children can use nonliteral language to capture the narrative structure of a pretend episode, not just to set it in motion.

FURTHER IMPLICATIONS

Before developing a theoretical account, it is helpful to highlight some important but less obvious findings. First, as noted earlier, the remarks made by the adult in Experiments 1 and 2 (e.g., "The cat wants some tea," or, "The pig wants some banana") could not be decoded literally: children needed to interpret them as making reference to make-believe entities.

Thus, they had to respond to the statements by treating them as a special category of performative (Austin, 1962). Like other types of performative (e.g., promising, threatening), their utterance served to bring about the state of affairs that they referred to. Thus, hearing a reference to "tea" or "banana," children needed to assume that the pretend world in which they were operating contained such entities. A theoretical account of the results should specify how children process such nonliteral performatives.

Second, 28-month-olds were good at adjusting their pretend action to the current make-believe status of the object: they were able to treat a stick first as a spoon and then as a toothbrush. In one respect, these results replicate the familiar observation that 2-year-olds can treat one object as a substitute for another. In addition, however, they highlight the fact that a pretend identity is appropriate only for a given pretend context. Once that context is set aside, the temporary pretend identity of the prop should also be set aside. The prop can then be either used for its normal function or ascribed a new pretend identity. The fact that 28-month-olds were able to assign two different pretend identities to the same object and rarely produced pretend responses inappropriate to the ongoing script shows that they understood this feature of pretense. Any theoretical account must explain not just how children ascribe a pretend identity to a prop but also how they circumscribe that ascription to the current pretend context.

Experiment 5 showed that children understand pretend transformations whose outcomes are invisible. Liquid was "poured," but, since it was imaginary, no surface became visibly messy. Toothpaste was "squirted," but no surface became visibly dirty. Presumably, children filled in these empty perceptual slots through causal extrapolation: they imagined that the floor had become "wet" or that the pig had become "dirty." The experiment illustrates a further point, however. Teddy mimed some of the components of the transformation: the toothpaste tube was applied to the pig's tail; the teapot was lifted and tilted. These displacements took place in a standard, visible fashion. Thus, if pretend "squirting" and pretend "pouring" are to be decoded appropriately by the child, they call for an admixture of perceptual analysis and imagination. Perceptual analysis is needed to determine the particular pretend action that is being carried out, but imagination is needed to extrapolate to the consequences.

The results of Experiments 6 and 7 revealed that 2-year-olds understand and produce nonliteral language. When asked, "What did Teddy do?" children realized that the adult was posing a question not about what Teddy had actually done—strictly speaking, he had merely lifted and manipulated various containers—but about what Teddy had pretended to do. In reply, they referred appropriately to Teddy's make-believe actions. The coordination of nonliteral language with pretend play raises an important theoretical question about how the child can simultaneously orchestrate two symbolic systems, using one system (i.e., language) to talk about the referents of the other system (i.e., a pretend episode).

In summary, 2-year-olds understand nonliteral questions and stipulations, treat make-believe stipulations in an appropriate, context-bound fashion, combine perceptual analysis and imagination when keeping track of pretend transformations, and coordinate two symbolic systems. In the next chapter, we offer a theoretical model of our main findings and these additional, less obvious results.

VII. A THEORETICAL MODEL

We may now start to construct a theoretical model of these various observations. We describe a model with two complementary features. First, we argue that pretense comprehension has striking analogies with text comprehension, particularly story comprehension. We pursue that analogy in four ways. (1) Children need to keep track of the pretend identity of make-believe props; similarly, in story comprehension, it is necessary to keep track of the identity of referring expressions. (2) A pretend episode, like a story episode, brings certain referents into focus, but this focus is temporary, lasting only for the duration of the episode. (3) Pretend comprehension, like story comprehension, calls for elaborative causal inferences that integrate successive parts of an episode. (4) Elaborative or constructive processing in the context of both pretense comprehension and story comprehension yields an interconnected, memorable representation of the episode.

The other feature of our theoretical model is a specification of the cognitive processes that underlie pretense comprehension. We argue that children label or "flag" props in the immediate vicinity in line with current make-believe stipulations. In the course of a given pretend episode, some flags require revision because the pretend status of particular props changes as the pretend episode unfolds. We refer to this updating process as "flag editing." We argue that "flagging" and "flag editing" can explain the four characteristics of pretense comprehension described above.

We introduce the model by working through each of the main findings reviewed in the previous chapter. We assume that the process of pretense comprehension is set in motion by signals that mark a shift from the reality to the pretense mode. Recall that our experiments typically started with a warm-up period in which toys and props were made available. In addition, the experimenter sometimes engaged in preliminary acts of pretending and encouraged the child to join in. We did not subject these preliminaries to experimental analysis, but we assume that they serve an important alerting function. They tell the child, "This is play" (Bateson, 1972; Mitchell, 1991), and they lead children to expect that subsequent episodes will include the special category of performatives that we have called "make-believe stipulations."

THE COMPREHENSION OF MAKE-BELIEVE STIPULATIONS

From the results of Experiment 1, we know that children interpret a reference to a nonexistent object as a make-believe stipulation of that object rather than as a deviant utterance. Thus, when the adult says, "Here's the cow. . . . You give the cow some tea," the child is not mystified by the absence of tea but treats the utterance as referring to imaginary tea inside the teapot.

We can elucidate the comprehension of such pretend utterances by considering the process of text comprehension among adults. Recent experimental work has shown that, in building a mental model of the speaker's meaning, the listener (or reader) must go beyond what is literally stated. In particular, the decoding of many referring statements calls for a constructive process. The listener uses information supplied by general knowledge, by previous discourse, or by the immediate context to identify the referent of a referring expression. For example, when readers encounter a sentence such as "The fish attacked the swimmer," they can begin to specify the particular type of fish from their general knowledge—they think of a predatory fish such as a shark, as shown by the ease with which they read a succeeding sentence like "The shark swam rapidly through the water" (Garnham, 1981). Alternatively, they can retrieve information supplied earlier in the text to identify the type of fish (Sanford & Garrod, 1981). Finally, when the utterance pertains to the immediate context ("*That* fish attacked the swimmer"), they can use it to identify the type of fish.

In each of these cases, comprehension calls for a constructive process of slot completion. The speaker mentions a referent, but the citation does not fully identify the referent. The specification is completed by the listener. We contend that the comprehension of pretend utterances calls for a similar process. Speakers in joint pretense use make-believe stipulations to introduce referents that are not actually present. The stipulation serves as a signal that there is a slot to be completed by the listener through a constructive act of pretense. Thus, within a pretend episode, a partner mentions a referent but underspecifies that referent, leaving the other partner to engage in slot completion. Slot completion consists in the identification of a relevant prop and a constructive act of pretense directed at that prop.

As noted, there are three primary modes of slot completion in text comprehension—via general knowledge, via the recovery of previously supplied information (i.e., the process of anaphora), and via recourse to the immediate context (i.e., the process of deixis). The same holds true for the comprehension of pretend utterances. For example, in Experiment 1, children could recruit their general knowledge that tea and cereal can be found in distinctive containers to select the stipulated container. When the adult invited them to give one of the test animals some cake in Experiment 2, they could rely, in anaphoric fashion, on a previously stipulated link between a particular type of prop and cake. In Experiment 7, they could interpret the adult's remark, "Let's give him some sausage," by referring to the immediate context: the adult was simultaneously placing a piece of Play-Doh on a paper plate.

Having identified the prop, the child needs to engage in the pretense specified by the make-believe stipulation and to store this pretend information for future reference. This enables partners in a game of make-believe to carry over pretend stipulations concerning a given prop into later parts of the pretend episode. We introduce the "flagging" process to specify how pretend stipulations are mentally represented. We assume that children store a mental flag that indicates the relevant prop(s) (e.g., yellow brick[s] or a teapot) and the (make-believe) identity or contents of these props (e.g., make-believe banana[s] or tea). Thus, a flag might bear the complete statement, "The teapot contains (make-believe) tea." The effect of these statements is straightforward. Whenever the child attends to or acts on the prop, they are read and used as a guide for action.

We may now consider how such flags are stored. In principle, children could store flags in three different ways; we evaluate the advantages and disadvantages of each. First, they could flag the specific prop whose identity or contents are stipulated in the speaker's statement. For example, children might attach a flag to their mental representation of the yellow brick that the adult has fed to the monkey. This flag would bear the statement, "This brick is a (make-believe) banana." Similarly, children might attach a flag to their mental representation of the teapot that reads, "This teapot contains (make-believe) tea." When they subsequently attend to the brick or teapot, the flag is retrieved and read, and thus the flagged item is treated appropriately.

Whatever its initial plausibility, such a prop-based flagging process cannot handle the results of Experiment 2. Children did not simply pretend that the particular block that the experimenter had handled was a banana; rather, they appropriately extrapolated to other yellow bricks, feeding them to animals who allegedly liked bananas. In the model just proposed, no such extrapolation can occur since flags are attached only to particular props.

A second mode of storage offers a solution to this problem: instead of storing a flag with a mental representation of a particular prop in the immediate environment, children might attach the flag to their mental representation of the *category* that the particular prop belongs to. For example, a flag might read, "Objects that belong to this category [i.e., yellow brick] are (make-believe) bananas." Now whenever a yellow brick is categorized as such, there will be a mental flag attached to the mental representation of that category that serves as a reminder to pretend that the object in question is a banana.

However, such a flagging operation will have dangerous cognitive consequences, as Leslie (1987) has pointed out. If children relabel their mental categories, there is a risk of abusing those categories. If they begin to think of bricks as bananas, conceptual confusion will ensue. Even if they remember that the bricks are only make-believe bananas (as the flag stipulates), confusion will occur once the game of pretend is over. In the real world, bricks are not make-believe bananas. Leslie's solution to this problem is to propose that children make duplicates of potentially threatened concepts. They edit a "decoupled" copy of their mental concept rather than its original. The copy can be edited for the purpose of pretend play, whereas the original remains intact.

There is, however, a simpler solution that simultaneously avoids the problem of overly restricted flagging mentioned earlier as well as the danger of representational abuse. We propose that children attach a flag neither to a mental representation of a specific prop nor to the mental representation of a prop's category but simply to a mental representation of the current pretend episode. That flag can refer to an isolated prop or to a set of props. For example, in the former case, the flag might read, "During this episode, this teapot contains (make-believe) tea." In the latter case, the flag might read, "During this episode, yellow bricks are (make-believe) bananas." In effect, the child allows the flagging process to operate only within the context of a particular make-believe episode.

This episode-based flagging is more wide ranging than that implied by the first hypothesis but less potent (and potentially damaging) than that implied by the second. It has two key advantages. First, unlike the first hypothesis, it can explain the process of extrapolation observed in Experiment 2: a stipulation can apply to a particular prop, but it can also be extended to all available items of a given category for the duration of the pretend episode. Second, unlike the second hypothesis, it need have no recourse to a complex copying and decoupling process to rescue children from the danger of representational abuse. Once a particular pretend episode is over, the flags that attach to it will be unread and ineffectual.

One final advantage may be mentioned. In saying that flags cease to be read, we do not mean that they are deleted or erased from memory. Rather, we assume that they are entered into a long-term store together with the child's representation of the pretend episode. The flags lose their force because that representation ceases to operate in working memory. If children can be prompted to recall the pretend episode, we assume that flags associated with the episode will be retrieved and read once again.

PRODUCING APPROPRIATE PRETEND ACTIONS

The results of Experiments 3 and 4 highlighted two aspects of the 2-year-olds' competence: the ability to select a pretend action in terms of the stipulated, episode-bound identity of a prop and the ability to direct two different pretend actions toward the same prop in successive episodes.

The episode-bound flagging process described in the preceding section offers a straightforward explanation for both findings. When the child is asked by the experimenter to help Teddy with a given prop, the flagging process indicates the stipulated identity of that prop for the current episode. For example, depending on whether Teddy is getting ready for bed or eating his dinner, a block will have been flagged as a piece of soap or a sandwich. The child produces a pretend action guided by that flagged identity. In acting on the props, priority is given to the flagged statements rather than to the objective properties of the props. If the block is a make-believe sandwich, the child can pretend to feed it to Teddy; if the block is make-believe soap, the child can pretend to wash Teddy with it. Note that flags are used to guide pretend, not literal, actions. More generally, flags provide information only about what is true in the pretend world, not about the state of the real world. Thus, if a block is flagged as a make-believe sandwich, the flag warrants make-believe eating, not genuine eating.

Once an episode is completed, the flags associated with it cease to be read. The props are liberated from their stipulated identity and are available to assume a different identity in a subsequent episode. Hence, there is little likelihood of inappropriate pretense intrusions: a flag has no efficacy outside the pretend context in which it is planted. Again, we find an interesting analogy with discourse comprehension. Experimental work has shown that the discourse context that is currently being processed brings a set of referents into focus. Anaphor resolution remains relatively fast so long as the set of referents remains in focus. Given a change of context, the set of referents moves out of focus and slows anaphor resolution time (Lesgold, Roth, & Curtis, 1979). For example, Anderson, Garrod, and Sanford (1983) found that characters tied to a particular episode (e.g., waiters in restaurant settings) go out of focus at episode boundaries (e.g., when an incident taking place at the restaurant comes to an end) even though main characters remain in focus. Similarly, Morrow, Bower, and Greenspan (1990) found that items associated with a particular room went out of focus when the protagonist left for another room.

PRETEND CAUSAL TRANSFORMATIONS

So far, we have discussed how the child keeps track of the special status of props within the world of pretense using a process of episode-based prop flagging. We now consider how real-world general knowledge, particularly causal knowledge, is also recruited in order to edit and update existing flags. Editing and updating are required because the initial pretend situation is transformed as the action unfolds, creating a new pretend situation that must be captured by the flagging process.

In recruiting real-world knowledge, we assume that the child is constrained by the following general rule: whenever a prop is visibly acted on—for example, whenever it is moved or brought into contact with another object—that action calls for flag editing. Flags should be added in line with the causal transformations that would obtain if the objects mentioned in the flags had been acted on. For example, a flag might specify that a teapot contains make-believe tea. When that teapot is tilted, a flag for make-believe tea pouring from the spout must be written. Similarly, when a tube of toothpaste is squeezed, then a flag for the emerging, make-believe toothpaste must be written. Newly generated flags can, in turn, provide the basis for additional flags. The animal beneath the teapot will be described as "wet," and the target of the toothpaste will be described as "messy." New flags can update existing flags: a flag specifying that a cup contains make-believe tea must be updated to specify "empty" if the cup is knocked over. Indeed, the flagging process applies not only to the props and imaginary objects involved in a pretend transformation but also to the pretend actions that bring these transformations about. In the literal world, naughty Teddy merely lifts and tilts the teapot. In the pretend world, however, the fact that Teddy lifts and tilts a teapot containing make-believe tea means that Teddy is engaged in make-believe "pouring."

The appropriate format for these editing rules is not yet clear, but we may consider two different possibilities: an imagery-driven model and a propositional model. Suppose that flagged information is fed into and supplements the child's perception of ongoing events. Watching a teapot that contains pretend tea being tilted, the child visualizes tea coming out of the spout. Effectively, the child's perception of events uses flagged information to construct imagery that extrapolates from the visible event. Similarly, a good mime artist leads us to "see" the imaginary ball that he juggles or the imaginary banana that he peels and eats.

An alternative possibility is that flagged information triggers a propositional process rather than visual imagery. For example, watching the teapot being tilted, the child works out the causal effect of that motion on the liquid inside. The child does not "see" the displacement in his or her mind's eye but "knows" that it must occur.

Regardless of the format for the editorial process, we may underline once more the analogy with text or story comprehension. A story typically consists of a set of causally connected episodes. However, the narrative does not provide an explicit statement of every step in the causal chain: the detective smokes a cigarette, but we are not told how he lit it; the heroine goes to see him, but we are not told her means of transport. Yet, in each case, if the context requires it, we can infer appropriate enabling events or tools (Haviland & Clark, 1974; Johnson, Bransford, & Solomon, 1973).

PRETEND LANGUAGE

In Experiment 6, children reported that Teddy "poured tea" on the monkey and made him all "wet" as a result, whereas, strictly speaking, Teddy merely lifted the empty teapot in the air and tilted it. The flagging process and its editorial rules can explain these findings as follows. In responding to the experimenter's questions, children do not describe the props and actions literally but instead consult the statements written on the various flags that have been generated and edited in the course of the pretend episode.

However, this claim raises a further question. Consider the initial open-ended question posed by the experimenter: "What did Teddy do?" The flagging model offers an explanation of how children could provide a non-literal description, but it does not in itself explain why they opted to do so—in principle, they might have provided a literal description instead. Occasionally, children did respond in this fashion. For example, one child in Experiment 6 said that Teddy "put the teapot on Monkey's head," and in Experiment 7 one said that Teddy "put the teapot on the block." Such replies were, however, very rare; the majority of children treated the experimenter's question as a request for a nonliteral description. Two different interpretations of this bias may be considered. First, children may have stored two distinct mental representations of what they saw: a representation of what actually happened (e.g., "Teddy lifted the teapot, moved it to a position above the monkey, briefly tilted the spout downward, and then put it down again") and a representation of the pretend meaning of those events (e.g., "Teddy poured tea over the monkey and made him wet"). Both these representations would then be available when the experimenter asks what Teddy has done. However, since the experimenter's questions are posed immediately following the pretend episode, children infer that the experimenter is asking for a description of the pretend episode, not a literal account of what happened. An inference of this type is not implausible. In line with the maxim of relevance, it is appropriate to infer that the adult is posing a question that pertains to what has happened within the pretense frame (Sperber & Wilson, 1986).

However, we doubt that the two representations are equally available when the test questions are posed. It seems likely that the pretend representation is the one more readily available, and this biases the child to provide a nonliteral description in response to the adult's question. How might such differential availability arise? When children engage in constructive flagging, they produce a determinate, interconnected record of what they have seen. For example, if Teddy is about to "pour tea" from the teapot, it becomes significant that he moves it to a position above the monkey's head before doing so. His pouring tea in that position determines the identity of his victim and what will happen to his victim. By contrast, if Teddy's action is glossed in a literal fashion, its mode of execution is less obviously consequential. It is of no particular significance that Teddy holds the teapot above the monkey before tilting it because there are no consequences that draw the monkey into the episode when he does so.

From work on text processing, we know that a causally connected, coherent representation of a set of elements is more memorable than a disconnected representation of the same elements. For example, Bransford and Johnson (1972) and Dooling and Lachman (1971) showed that subjects are better able to recall a passage if they are supplied beforehand with a context that enables the elements to be coherently integrated. Moreover, within a narrative passage, events that are pivotal, and thereby enjoy causal connections in memory with many other events in the story, are especially well remembered (Myers & Duffy, 1990; Trabasso & Sperry, 1985; Trabasso & van den Broek, 1985). Thus, according to this second interpretation, the child who makes sense of Teddy's actions in a pretend mode will store an interconnected representation that will be more memorable than any literal encoding of the elements from which it is constructed. Causally pivotal events will be especially memorable. Hence, the child who responds to the adult's questions by describing the make-believe transformation that Teddy carried out is simply describing his or her dominant representation of what took place. By implication, if children were asked to state what Teddy had literally done, and only that, they might have difficulty. They remember that Teddy "poured tea" over the monkey, not that he "picked up the teapot, held it above the monkey's head, tilted it, and put it down again."

What, then, should we make of the fact that children did sometimes proffer a literal description in reply to the experimenter's initial question? One plausible interpretation is that, when they watched Teddy, they failed to create a nonliteral representation of his action. Thus, their response was not due to any misconstrual of the experimenter's question; rather, it faithfully reflected their representation of what happened.

In summary, our model of pretense comprehension treats a pretense episode as a text that must be subjected to constructive, inferential processing. We have emphasized four aspects of this analogy. First, in understanding pretend stipulations, children must make an appropriate mapping between manipulable props, such as a yellow brick or an empty teapot, and referents in the pretend world, such as "banana" or "tea." This mapping process is analogous to the mapping that occurs between referring expressions, such as "the fish," and particular referents in the story world, such as a predatory shark. We assume that such mappings are stored in the form of episode-bound flags. Second, the flagging process is tied to the current episode. The flagged statements lose their force once the episode is over; in the same way, discourse referents are brought into focus in an episode-bound fashion. Third, a complete causal chain is rarely fully specified by perception during a pretense episode. In order to understand what is being enacted, children must supplement what they see by making causal inferences. Similarly, text processing often calls for an inferential constructive process. Causes and consequences may be inferred, even when they are not explicitly stated. Fourth, the constructive processing of a pretense episode yields an interconnected representation in which causally pivotal events are especially memorable. Constructive processing of a text produces the same outcome.

CURRENT THEORIES OF PRETENSE

Having sketched a model of the comprehension process, we may compare its scope and assumptions with alternative theories of pretense. We organize our discussion around three alternative approaches: the symbolic theory of pretense, chiefly inspired by Piaget, and two more contemporary approaches.

Piaget's Theory

Following Piaget, most investigators have regarded pretend play as a form of symbolism. We shall argue that this approach is fruitful but that it has also led to an unhelpful denigration of the symbols of pretend play in comparison with the signs of language.

Because Piaget's account has been so influential, it is worth highlighting its main features. The original title of Piaget's (1951) monograph—*La formation du symbole*—indicates his theoretical approach explicitly. Pretend play is identified as part of a wide-ranging semiotic function that emerges in the course of the second year. Nonetheless, Piaget follows his compatriot Saussure in contrasting symbols (e.g., acts of pretense with props) with signs (e.g., language; Piaget, 1951, pp. 98–99). Consider the well-known observations of Jacqueline, who acts as if a cloth, and eventually the tail of a toy donkey, were a pillow. In Piaget's terms, Jacqueline treats the tail as a symbol—it serves as a signifier whose referent (or signified) is the absent pillow. Piaget underlines the inadequacy of such symbols in comparison with linguistic signs in which there is a genuinely arbitrary relation between signifier and signified (i.e., between sound and meaning). That relation is maintained by the conventions of the language-speaking community. By contrast, the props of pretend play are selected, not because of social convention, but because of some iconic similarity to the objects that they represent. Admittedly, in the course of development, the child's reliance on iconic similarity wanes, and more arbitrary object substitutions are accepted, but, according to Piaget, the symbols of pretend play retain their idiosyncratic, aconventional aspect. Thus, Piaget's account of pretense is castigatory in tone: symbolic play aspires toward but falls short of the fully fledged arbitrariness of signs as exemplified by language.

We shall argue that Piaget's tendency to see pretense as an inferior semiotic mode leads him to ignore or undervalue three distinctive features of pretend play: pretend transformations, the use of nonliteral language, and the fictional status of pretense.

Pretend Transformation

We concur with Piaget in regarding pretend play as a type of symbolism different from language, but we do not think that it is helpful to characterize it as inferior. Because symbolic substitutions involve material objects, they serve as a vehicle for implications that cannot be conveyed in the same way by using language. For example, when a statue signifies an ideology, operations on the signifier carry implications for the signified. The erection of Lenin's statue in the Baltic states is tantamount to an extension of the ideology's dominion. A deliberate dismantling of that same statue constitutes a rejection of the ideology. Similarly, if a piece of Play-Doh signifies a sausage, handing over a piece of Play-Doh is tantamount to handing over a serving of sausage. Pouring milk or even pretend milk on the Play-Doh ruins the sausage.

Admittedly, the transformation of a statue is intended to convey a serious ideological change, not a make-believe change. Nevertheless, in each of these examples, an equivalent semiotic mechanism is at work. An observer can understand what is being conveyed if the transformations of the signifier are regarded as having implications for the signified. Our notion of flagging and editing is intended to capture the way in which ploys directed at the signifier (dismantling a statue, handing over a piece of Play-Doh) are transposed into the signified world (an ideology, a sausage).

Note that this kind of semiotic transposition is impossible for a linguistic sign. The spoken word cannot be materially acted on and modified in the same way as a physical prop such as a statue or a piece of Play-Doh. It can be modified only by the selection or addition of other signs (e.g., euphemisms, modifiers, etc.). At most, it is possible to alter the sound of a given word (e.g., through amplification or elision). Yet such modifications carry no implication for the concept signified. To the extent that Piaget saw pretend props as an inferior forerunner of the genuinely arbitrary signs of language, he ignored this generative and distinctive feature of pretense play with props. Neo-Piagetian approaches have also neglected the distinctive semiotic nature of symbolic play, stressing instead parallels between the emergence of symbolic play and language (Bates, Benigni, Bretherton, Camaione, & Volterra, 1979; Fein, 1981; McCune-Nicolich, 1981).

Nonliteral Language

Piaget's account of the symbolic nature of pretend play does not explain the use of language within pretend play. Consider an adult's statement (in Experiment 7) that the monkey loves chocolate, which was uttered as the monkey was given a block on a paper plate. If the child treats the word "chocolate" as an ordinary linguistic sign, he or she will be mystified because no genuine chocolate is present. On the other hand, it will not help to regard the word "chocolate" as a symbol: it bears no iconic similarity to its referent (i.e., a brown block). Similar remarks can be made, mutatis mutandis, about the production of nonliteral language by the child.

A solution to this impasse can be reached if we acknowledge that language used in the context of pretend play has a hybrid status. It combines certain features of ordinary linguistic signs with those of symbolic props. Thus, although the word "chocolate" retains its standard, literal sense in the context of pretend play, it can be used to refer, in a nonstandard fashion, to a brown block if the block is serving temporarily as a symbolic prop for chocolate. Interestingly, Piaget remarks briefly on the use of verbal signs within pretend play. For example, at 19 months, Jacqueline says "[s]avon" (soap) as she pretends to wash her hands. Yet, despite such observations, Piaget goes on to reiterate the conceptual dichotomy between signs and symbols.

The account that we have given indicates how children might grasp the hybrid status of pretend language. Effectively, they must coordinate their standard use of linguistic signs with the flagging process. The flagging process permits the creation of a representation that serves as a bridge or mediator between language and the perceptible gestures and props that make up a pretense episode.

This mediation can operate bidirectionally. On the one hand, the child who watches a pretend episode can create a pretend representation and then use that representation to talk about the pretend episode. For example, the child who watches an adult tilt a teapot above a brick can construct a representation of what this gesture means in terms of pretense—that is, flag that "the (make-believe) chocolate is now (make-believe) wet"—and then use that representation to construct a linguistic description of what has happened, as in Experiment 7.

Processing operates in the reverse direction when the child hears an adult produce a nonliteral statement. The child listens to an adult make an utterance during pretend play and uses that utterance to construct a pretend representation by flagging the episode currently under way. For example, in Experiment 7, the adult offered a prop to a toy animal and simultaneously provided a linguistic gloss, saying, "The monkey likes to eat chocolate. Let's give him some chocolate." We assume that children treated this statement as a stipulation of the pretend identity of the block and flagged it accordingly.

The Fictional Status of Pretense

In his discussion of pretense substitutions, Piaget describes how an action outside its ordinary context (putting one's head on a cloth) can stand for an action in its ordinary context (putting one's head on a pillow). Although Piaget is at pains to stress the playful aspect of pretense, his analysis explicitly states that pretense is initially used to signify reality. The child who is pretending to go to sleep signifies thereby the real act of going to sleep (Piaget, 1951, p. 101).

At a later stage, Piaget does acknowledge that the child uses pretense to represent nonexistent or fictional episodes or characters. For example, Piaget reports that J. (aged 28 months) pretended to carry out activities that she was not allowed to engage in (e.g., carrying her baby sister). At 47 months, she invented a hybrid creature ("aseau") whom she imitated by pretending to crawl and fly. Yet Piaget insists that even these more advanced pretend activities are ultimately tied to reality: "The striking feature of these symbolic combinations is the extent to which the child reproduces or continues the real world, the imaginative symbol being only a means to increase his range, not an end in itself. In reality, the child has no imagination, and what we ascribe to him as such is no more than a lack of coherence, and still more, subjective assimilation" (Piaget, 1951, p. 131). Thus, Piaget implies repeatedly that pretense is a tool, and a poor one at that, for the assimilation of reality. As Bretherton (1984) has emphasized, Piaget was reluctant to see symbolic play as an intellectually progressive activity. Indeed, he argued that symbolic play is discarded when the child can accommodate more effectively to reality.

Piaget's analysis conflates two separate issues: the inspiration for an act of pretense and the status of what is thereby signified. Piaget is probably correct to insist that real events in the child's life are often reenacted in a distorted form during make-believe play. However, that does not show that the child is incapable of enacting a genuinely fictional episode. Shakespeare's *Antony and Cleopatra* is inspired by (and is a partial distortion of) actual events, but it is just as much a piece of dramatic fiction as *King Lear* or *Othello*.

Admittedly, a pretense action can sometimes be intended to signify a real action. For example, a child can pretend to be asleep on Christmas Eve, in the hope of glimpsing Santa Claus. In this case, however, the child is pretending to be asleep in order to convey to Santa Claus that he or she is really asleep. The situation is different in symbolic play. Here, the child lies down on a cloth in order to convey—within the fictional episode currently under way—that he or she is asleep. At 18 months, the episode might stop at this point, but somewhat later it can be incorporated into a more elaborate fictional episode. Whatever the complexity of the surrounding episode, the key point is that, during pretense, a signifier (lying down, closing the eyes momentarily) does not signify the real act of sleeping. Even though it may be inspired by and a partially accurate reproduction of the real act of sleeping, it can still be a piece of make-believe in that it stands for a fictional act of sleeping. In the same way, a child who plays the role of mother might incorporate into that pretense some of her mother's familiar words and phrases. She may nevertheless be engaged in a piece of make-believe— playing the part of a (fictional) mother, not pretending to be her own mother.

This claim becomes all the more plausible if we consider children's pretend language once more, as assessed in Experiments 6 and 7. When children talk about the imaginary substance that Teddy poured or squeezed onto his victims, or when they talk about the imaginary outcome of what Teddy did, it is clear that they are referring to fictional substances and fictional outcomes. It would be misleading to say that they are using the words "toothpaste" or "wet" to refer to real substances and real outcomes. If that were their intention, they would radically misunderstand the nature of pretense.

More generally, we conclude that the emergence of symbolic play is highly significant for the child's cognitive development. It is not an activity by which reality is reproduced and distorted; it offers the child an initial entry into the world of fiction and of drama. Nor should pretend play be seen as an inferior symbolic activity. It marks the conjunction of two powerful semiotic systems: the stipulation and transformation of props and the nonliteral use of language.

Contemporary Alternatives

Recent interest in the child's theory of mind (Astington et al., 1988) has been accompanied by renewed theorizing about the nature of pretense. We consider two different approaches and compare them to our own.

Leslie's Theory

Leslie (1987, 1988b) develops a systematic account of the representational nature of pretense. His starting point is what he calls the danger of "representational abuse." Consider a child who pretends that a banana is a telephone or watches a sibling pretending that a banana is a telephone. One way for the child to represent this pretend link is to connect two ordinary mental concepts—the concept for banana and the concept for telephone. However, these conceptual connections are dangerous. If the concept of bananas is extended to include the concept of telephones, then both concepts will be overextended.

Although Leslie does not refer to it, Saussure's (1916/1983) distinction between symbols and signs is pertinent. The threat of representational abuse arises in pretend play precisely because its signifiers (e.g., bananas) are objects in their own right. In the case of language, by contrast, the signifiers are not objects in their own right. A word is not an object with an inherent identity and function. In using pretend props, however, children need simultaneously to preserve their conceptual knowledge of the identity and function of the signifier (e.g., a banana) and to allow it to stand for the signified (e.g., a telephone).

To explain how representational abuse is avoided, Leslie borrows a computer metaphor. Children engaged in pretense—or watching another person so engaged—do not operate on files or entries in their primary conceptual system. These are reserved for dealing with the world as it really is. Instead, they create a copy of a relevant entry in the primary system, mark the copy as such with a distinctive notation, and perform mental operations on that copy. Since the copy is separated, or "decoupled," from its original in the primary system by its distinctive notation, these mental operations do not abuse entries in the primary system.

To take a concrete example, having made a copy of a primary entry for an empty cup on the table and marked it as a copy, the child can attach to that copy the claim that the cup contains tea. Although the cup is actually empty, no harm is done because that real-world information remains safe and untouched in the primary system. Similarly, having made a copy of an entry for a toy horse, the child can add the claim that it is galloping without harming the information (stored in the primary system) that toy horses do not gallop.

Leslie completes the decoupling model with several additional computational steps. Decoupled statements such as "This (empty) cup contains tea" are linked to particular agents adopting particular propositional attitudes. For example, when engaged in joint play, the child might represent the fact that either the play partner or the self is pretending that the cup contains tea. According to Leslie, the child can recognize that pretending is a particular mental attitude tied to a particular agent. By implication, the 2-year-old is capable of metarepresentation: the ability to represent a mental state such as pretending.

Once created, decoupled expressions can also be informed and updated on the basis of real-world causal knowledge. For example, if the child is pretending that a cup has tea in it, and if the cup is knocked over, knowledge of what happens when a cup is upturned can be recruited to predict what will happen to the pretend tea. Finally, newly created or updated expressions can be used to guide actions in the real world. Having represented the fact that a particular cup has pretend tea in it, the child can pick it up to engage in pretend drinking or tip its pretend contents over a play partner.

The account that we have proposed has several important affinities with Leslie's. In contrast to earlier theoretical accounts, but in sympathy with Leslie, we have stressed the role of pretense comprehension. Second, we are also impressed by the ease with which children recruit their real-world causal knowledge to make predictions and inferences within a pretend world. Finally, we agree that it is necessary to avoid the danger of representational abuse: claims that hold true within the world of pretense must not be permitted to infiltrate claims about the real world.

Despite this agreement on general theoretical goals, our proposed solutions differ in three important ways. First, Leslie postulates that copies are made of conceptual entries in the primary system so that any editing of such copies may leave the original untouched. This procedure is aimed at forestalling the danger of representational abuse in the primary conceptual system. We argue instead that pretend statements do not lead to abuse because they are stored along with the representation of the pretend episode. Such flagged statements remain unread and therefore innocuous once the episode is over—although they can be read again if the episode is reinstated. Indeed, we would argue that, by starting from a copy of a primary entry, the decoupling model creates conceptual problems rather than solving them. A copy of a primary entry will include primary features of the prop (e.g., the yellow color of the banana) that are irrelevant to, or in conflict with, the pretense that is enacted (e.g., pretending that it is a telephone). These features must then be deleted. If deletions are not made, logical contradictions may ensue within the pretend frame. Suppose, for example, that the child notices an empty cup and makes a copy of his or her mental representation of this entity, marking it as a decoupled entry with the help of mental quotation marks—"this empty cup." If the child now modifies this copy by adding a further specification, suitable for the pretend episode in hand, he or she might arrive at the following—"this empty cup contains tea." (This example is borrowed from Leslie, 1987, p. 420.) Thus, the child ends up pretending that the cup both is empty and contains liquid. Leslie (1988a) half recognizes this problem, noting that it would be illogical to pretend that a cup is both empty and full of liquid. Yet inspection of Leslie's theoretical proposals (Leslie, 1987, 1988b) shows that they contain no deletion process and produce exactly such logical contradictions. In fact, the child is pretending that the cup, which happens to be empty, contains liquid, and this is captured by the flagging process but not by the decoupling process. In the flagging process, the child stores a flag that reads, "During this episode, this cup contains (make-believe) tea." Since a copying or "decoupling" process is not used, the information in the primary system that the cup is actually empty does not figure in the pretend statement and does not require deletion to avoid contradiction.

We can highlight the difference between decoupling and flagging in the following way. Decoupling starts from a prop such as a cup or banana; by a series of computational steps that include copying and editing the conceptual entry for that prop, it eventually arrives at a decoupled statement that specifies the pretend contents or identity of the prop. Flagging works in the opposite direction; it starts from a pretend stipulation, and that stipulation is directed at a prop or set of props within the immediate situation.

A second difference concerns the degree of psychological insight implied by the two accounts. Leslie builds into the 2-year-old a fully fledged appreciation of the mental attitude of the pretender, be it another person or the self. Thus, he proposes that "exactly the same mechanism will account for both the ability to pretend oneself and the ability to understand pretense in others" (Leslie, 1988b, p. 29) and that pretense comprehension involves "attributing a mental state" to the pretender (Leslie, 1988b, p. 23). It is easy to overlook the radical nature of this conjecture. Consider, briefly, other propositional attitudes such as "think," "want," or "fear." Recent work on the child's conception of mind has insisted on the crucial importance of distinguishing between two levels of sophistication. A 12-month-old child might reasonably be said to think, desire, or fear that a particular situation is about to occur; but, while entertaining these propositional attitudes, the child does not self-consciously realize and represent his or her own mental states. Only later do children represent—and talk about—their own mental states. In short, the ability to adopt a propositional attitude is not equivalent to having a conception—or theory—about that attitude. Virtually all commentators have acknowledged this decalage, although they disagree about how it should be conceptualized and how long it lasts (e.g., Chandler, 1988; Olson, Astington, & Harris, 1988; Perner, 1991; Wellman, 1990). Leslie's model effectively collapses this important distinction, implying that the ability to engage in pretense emerges at the same time as the ability to represent that someone, be it self or other, is engaged in the mental state of pretending.

Our model is much more conservative. We anticipate that children might be able to engage in pretense, including joint pretense, without diagnosing the mental state of their play partner or of themselves. Rather, they interpret and accept a set of stipulations about the current make-believe situation. In our model, the flagged statements do not record the state of mind of any particular player—they state what should be taken as (fictionally) true of the current situation. The adult acts as if a particular situation were true; the child's task is not to understand the mental state of the adult but to figure out what that make-believe situation is and to act in concert.

This is not to deny, of course, that the child can distinguish the contribution of individual players to the make-believe situation. For example, in Experiment 3, the children presumably knew that it was the experimenter who squeezed make-believe toothpaste (in the first episode of the bedtime script). In Experiments 6 and 7, children's replies showed that they knew that it was Teddy who squeezed make-believe toothpaste. Our point is that children need make no inferences about the mental state of the experimenter or of Teddy (whatever that might be) in understanding their actions. All they need to understand is that the adult or Teddy is squeezing make-believe toothpaste, not real toothpaste. To the extent that children distinguish between these two types of action, they understand that make-believe play involves pretend actions, but that understanding need not be based on a diagnosis of the mental state that underlies such actions.

This brings us to the final, and perhaps the most wide-ranging, difference between Leslie's model and our own. Leslie sees pretense as the emergence of a new type of logical machinery for dealing with the alleged opacity of pretend assertions. By contrast, we have attempted to relate our interpretation to a wider body of work on text processing. We find that linkage congenial because we see pretend play as the child's first entry into the world of fiction rather than as the emergence of a new logical capacity. This orientation warrants further discussion, which we provide in a concluding section.

Perner's Theory

On the basis of Piaget's observations of pretense, it is clear that children of about 18 months can differentiate between two distinct situations: the real situation, in which, for example, the object that Jacqueline is lying on is a cloth, and the make-believe situation, in which the cloth is treated as if it were a pillow. Perner accepts the general claim made by Leslie (1987) that differentiation between these situations must be guided by two distinct types of mental representation—one specifying the real world and the other specifying the make-believe or "as-if" world.

Nonetheless, Perner (1991) dissents from the theories advanced by both Piaget (1951) and Leslie (1987). He argues that the child simply represents two different situations, one being the real situation (e.g., "This object is a piece of cloth") and one being a hypothetical or as-if situation (e.g., "This object is my pillow"). In carrying out an act of pretense, the child switches control (knowingly, not by mistake) from the real situation to the hypothetical situation.

Against Piaget, Perner argues that early pretense does not call for a symbolic code. He proposes that, when Jacqueline puts her head on a cloth and pretends to go to sleep, she is treating the cloth as if it were a pillow, but she is not treating it as a symbol for a pillow. More generally, if Jacqueline were able to acknowledge that the cloth represents or symbolizes her pillow, she would be capable of metarepresentation, and Perner argues that metarepresentation can be achieved only much later.

In defending his assertion that early pretense does not involve symbolic substitution, Perner refers to Goodman's (1976) claim that genuine symbols represent the signified as having certain properties or relations. However, our results show that 2-year-olds meet Goodman's criterion. Children understand that objects can be used to represent the signified as having certain properties or relations. Consider the results of Experiment 7. Children described how Teddy's action on the substitute object had rendered the object that it signified wet or dirty. Thus, they realized that the substitute object represented the signified as having certain properties, meeting the criterion that Goodman advances. Similarly, in Experiment 7, they described Teddy's action on the empty container as pouring or putting its pretend contents "on" or "over" the substitute object. Accordingly, they thought of the pretend contents as being in a specific spatial relation with the substitute object, again meeting Goodman's criterion. Thus, although we agree with Perner that pretend play illustrates the children's capacity to represent hypothetical or as-if situations, we would argue that children understand how such situations can be symbolized by means of props and their transformations.

Finally, we may consider another skeptical claim made by Perner (in press), this time against Leslie's (1987) proposal that pretense calls for metarepresentation. In Leslie's account—as we described earlier—not only do children represent the pretend state of affairs, but they also diagnose the state of mind of the person engaged in pretense. Thus, the child mentally represents, not just that the cup contains make-believe tea, but also that it is the other person, the self, or both, who is adopting the mental attitude of pretending that the cup contains tea.

We share Perner's doubts that 2-year-olds engage in metarepresentation, but our reasons are different. Perner argues that an understanding of representation—which he regards as a prerequisite for metarepresentation—emerges only around 4 years of age. We doubt that 2-year-olds engage in metarepresentation on the grounds that they can understand that someone is pretending without diagnosing the person's mental attitude. As we argued earlier, when someone engages in pretend play by acting (and talking) as if a particular hypothetical situation were true, the child's task is to understand this fictional situation. The child does not have to identify the mental attitude of the play partner. Admittedly, the child might realize that the person is engaged in pretend play rather than acting seriously. However, that realization can be based on the relation between the person's actions (or utterances) and the type of situation that he or she directs those actions toward. Serious, nonpretend pouring is directed at real tea. By contrast, pretend pouring and references to make-believe tea are directed at empty teapots or empty teacups. Thus, in agreement with Lillard (1992), we would argue that, when children recognize that someone is pouring make-believe liquid rather than real liquid, they are recognizing a distinctive form of action rather than a distinctive mental stance of pretending.

In sum, we accept Perner's initial claim that, when young children engage in pretend play, they mentally represent a hypothetical or fictional situation. Moreover, although they recognize that the situation is a fictional "as-if" situation and can collaborate with another person in its stipulation and elaboration, we agree (for somewhat different reasons) that they are not capable of metarepresentation. However, contrary to Perner, we also believe that 2-year-olds realize that fictional episodes are constructed by means of symbols. A prop can serve as a symbol: a yellow brick can signify a banana, and a piece of Play-Doh can signify a sausage; the tilting of a teapot can signify pouring, and the raising of a spoon to the mouth can signify feeding. The fact that pretense includes actions directed at symbolic props—causing the "sausage" to become "wet"—does not show that pretense is a nonsymbolic medium. It shows only that the semiotics of pretend play are different from those of language. Nonetheless, in each medium, it is possible to represent an object as having certain properties or relations, meeting Goodman's (1976) criterion.

FUTURE RESEARCH

We have tried to show that children's understanding of pretense can be investigated and that it reveals a surprising competence even among young 2-year-olds. We now consider several directions for future research, beginning with predictions tied directly to our theoretical model.

Predictions of the Flagging Model

In describing the flagging model, we argued that new flags are written when the child observes an action that transforms a make-believe substance. We proposed that such newly generated flags can in turn trigger the writing of still further flags if the child observes an additional transformation. In the experiments described, children saw only a single causal transformation, such as liquid being poured from a container, but more complex, sequential transformations can be readily devised.

Suppose children watch while Teddy pours either make-believe talcum powder or make-believe juice into a neutral container and then pours the make-believe contents of the neutral container over his victim. In order to infer the outcome of the second pouring (i.e., from the neutral container), children must attend to the first, infer its outcome, and use that flag in inferring the outcome of the second: that Teddy's victim is covered in make-believe powder or juice.

A second and related prediction is that children should be able to infer the type of pretend action that is being enacted by reference to previously planted flags. For example, suppose that cotton wool inside a container is stipulated as either milk or ice cream. If Teddy now inverts the container in his customary mischievous fashion, he is "pouring" milk in the first case but "dropping" ice cream in the second.

A third prediction concerns the conditions under which pretend outcomes are inferred. In understanding text, an inference is especially likely if it is needed to integrate current input with earlier input. Consider the following pair of sentences: "No longer able to control his anger, the husband threw the delicate porcelain vase against the wall. It cost him well over one hundred dollars to replace the vase." An inference about what happened to the vase is optional after the first sentence but required after the second if the second sentence is to be integrated with the first. Consistent with this, subjects named a probe word ("broke") faster after reading the sentence pair than a control pair in which such a bridging inference was not required (Potts, Keenan, & Golding, 1988).

Our assumption that a pretend episode is processed in a text-like fashion leads to the prediction that bridging inferences are especially likely to be triggered if they ensure coherence between a later pretend action and an earlier one. In developing a concrete experimental proposal, it is helpful to recall the results of Experiments 6 and 7: when first asked what Teddy had done, children rarely mentioned the consequence of Teddy's action (e.g., that the animal or the food was "wet," "dirty," and so forth). Nevertheless, they could infer that consequence because they named it when explicitly asked in follow-up questions. We conclude that children probably did not infer the consequence as they watched Teddy but were prompted to do so by the experimenter's questions. If, however, Teddy's pretend action were followed by a remedial action contingent on the outcome of that action (e.g., another animal "dries" or "cleans" Teddy's victim), an inference concerning the outcome would be called for retrospectively, to make sense of the remedial action. Hence, it should be mentioned spontaneously when children are asked what Teddy did.

Finally, we may consider children's long-term memory for pretend episodes. We claimed that flags are not erased from memory but stored together with the pretend episode. Hence, we would predict that children who are presented with a prompt that is strongly associated with an earlier pretend episode should be able to reinstate, and be guided by, those flags once again. For example, in the episodes that were presented in Experiments 6 and 7, naughty Teddy played a central role and should serve as an effective prompt. Hence, children who watch Teddy pour make-believe tea on a substitute item (e.g., a yellow brick that has been stipulated as a banana) should be prompted to recall that episode, and its associated flags, if they are simply shown Teddy once again on the following day. If he now squeezes make-believe toothpaste on the "banana," they should be able to understand what he has done even if an explicit stipulation of the make-believe identity of the yellow brick is not provided. Children who receive no such reminder—they watch an unfamiliar character squeeze make-believe toothpaste on the "banana"—should have more difficulty reinstating the relevant flags.

The Comprehension and Production of Pretense

Theories about the development of pretense play have been chiefly based on the spontaneous production of pretense by the solitary child. Our studies of pretense comprehension offer an opportunity to compare production with comprehension. We first consider that relation from a psychometric standpoint.

In the case of language, measures of competence based on spontaneous production are relatively unproblematic because recording can be unobtrusive, extended over long periods of time, and readily transcribed. These conditions are much less easy to realize with respect to the production of pretense. To the extent that short bouts of pretense are studied (on either a cross-sectional or a longitudinal basis), there is a risk of underestimating a child's range or maximum performance.

Comprehension measures are more likely to provide a valid assessment of pretense competence since even a simple choice response may be sufficient to indicate comprehension of an extended pretense episode. Comprehension measures may prove particularly useful in the assessment of delayed or deviant groups. Consider, for example, the case of autism. It has long been asserted that autistic children play in a stereotypical fashion. Indeed, Leslie (1987) treats that deficit as a major target for his "decoupling" explanation of autism. However, Lewis and Boucher (1988) have argued for a motivational explanation. They report that, if prompted, autistic children will pretend; any deficit that they exhibit is restricted to the spontaneous production of pretend play. One way to resolve this controversy is to examine comprehension: the "decoupling" model predicts deficits in comprehension as well as production, whereas the motivational account does not.

From a theoretical standpoint, one might expect the comprehension of pretense to emerge in advance of production by analogy with the acquisition of language (Clark, 1983). However, our findings give, as yet, no basis for assuming such a decalage. Even if a decalage (in either direction) were found, it would not automatically follow that the critical flag-writing and -editing process differs radically between the two. Processes extrinsic to the flagging mechanism might account for the relative difficulty of comprehension as compared to production. Indeed, as Pinker has argued with respect to the acquisition of language (Pinker, 1984), it may be most fruitful to think of such rules as neutral with respect to comprehension and production. Adopting that approach, it is reasonable to predict that many of the sequences found for pretense production will be duplicated in the case of comprehension, even if the two sequences do not emerge in perfect synchrony.

Age Changes in the Comprehension of Pretense

In Experiments 1–5, children younger than 2 years were compared with young 2-year-olds. Several age changes emerged. As compared with 2-year-olds, children younger than 2 years were less likely to pour from the correct container in Experiment 1, extrapolate systematically to unused props in Experiment 2, show dual usage of props in Experiments 3 and 4, and direct their pretend action to the transformed prop in Experiment 5.

A consistent age difference also emerged in Experiments 6 and 7, in which younger and older 2-year-olds were compared. Younger 2-year-olds were less articulate than older 2-year-olds in responding to the initial open-ended question. They were less likely to mention Teddy's action, its direction, and the imaginary substance.

Our theoretical model helps us identify the potential cause of these age changes. In particular, it highlights the potential effect of age changes at three possible stages of pretend processing: during a make-believe stipulation (i.e., flag writing); during a causal transformation (flag editing); and, finally, when generating a pretend response (guided by the output of flag writing and editing).

The age change observed in Experiments 1–4 might have occurred either during the initial stage of flag writing or when generating a pretend response (note that children were not presented with any causal transformations in these four experiments so that flag editing was unnecessary). In future studies, it should be possible to locate the cause of the age change by simplifying the response required. For example, children can be asked to point to a given prop, named in terms of its script-based identity, rather than to generate a pretend action. If a comparable age change were found on such pointing tasks, it would imply that the initial script-based flag writing is difficult for children younger than 2 years, even when response production demands are minimal. Conversely, if the age change disappears, we may conclude that it is the generation of a pretend response that is problematic for children younger than 2 years even though initial flag writing proceeds smoothly.

With respect to Experiment 5, the age change might have occurred at all three processing stages: in recognizing the contents of the pretend containers (flag writing); in following the causal transformation (flag editing); or in generating the required pretend response. Again, strategic simplification should help locate the exact source of difficulty. Thus, children can be asked simply to point to a container containing a pretend substance (i.e., so that only flag writing is required) or alternatively to point to an object transformed by that pretend substance (i.e., so that flag writing and editing are required).

Finally, the age change found in Experiments 6 and 7 is almost certainly due to the stage of response generation and more specifically to the greater verbal fluency of older 2-year-olds. It is unlikely that any age difference occurred in flag writing or editing during presentation of the pretend episode because no systematic age changes were found in replies to the more explicit follow-up questions. Yet correct replies required an understanding of the pretend episodes.

Causal Reasoning

Experiments 5–7 demonstrated 2-year-olds' ability to make causal predictions. Children's actions and nonliteral descriptions were guided by an understanding of the (invisible) outcomes that Teddy had brought about. In analyzing the results of these three experiments, we presupposed such causal knowledge, focusing instead on children's understanding of pretend transformations. However, it is feasible to reverse the conceptual lens—to use children's understanding of pretense as a tool to assess their understanding of physical and psychological causation. To the extent that the outcome of a pretend transformation is invisible, it calls for an appropriate prediction from the child. Thus, pretend play might serve as a useful vehicle for the analysis of children's causal concepts, particularly since the sequence completion technique that is currently in use (Das Gupta & Bryant, 1989; Gelman, Bullock, & Meck, 1980) would be difficult to extend to children younger than 3 years.

Children's causal understanding in Experiments 5–7 highlights a further aspect of pretense. Although it is tempting to see much of early pretend play as the reenactment of familiar scripts and routines, we deliberately introduced episodes that deviated from a familiar script. Nonetheless, children's causal understanding enabled them to appreciate what had happened. To that extent, children's pretense comprehension is more flexible than the script concept would imply.

Nonliteral Language

One of our most unexpected and striking results was the facility with which 2-year-olds used nonliteral language. They used it to refer to imaginary states—the fact that an animal had been made "wet" or "messy" by Teddy's misdemeanors. They used it to refer to imaginary substances— "tea," "toothpaste," "paint," "glue," etc. And they used it to refer to substitute objects in terms of their pretend rather than their literal identity.

The latter usage is perhaps the most remarkable. Reference to an imaginary state or substance is not radically different from reference to a temporarily invisible object or to a missing but desired object. In each case, the terms can be used in the normal way despite the absence of any perceptible referent. By contrast, when the child talks about a prop in terms of its stipulated rather than its actual identity, normal usage must be overridden. For example, the child must temporarily ignore the standard terms for the prop in question (e.g., "block" or "Play-Doh").

These findings undermine the claim that children cannot represent an object in two different ways. For example, the fact that children do not solve the appearance-reality task has been interpreted as showing that children cannot simultaneously entertain two different representations of a given object. Thus, Flavell (1988), writing about 2–3-year-olds, states that "it makes no sense to them to hear something described as being radically different than the single way it 'is' (with 'is' not differentiated from 'seems to them at the moment')" (p. 245). Yet the children in our studies both understood and used descriptions that did not match the actual properties or identity of the object in question.

Woolley and Wellman (1990) point out that many of the stimuli used by Flavell are deceptive: they initially appear to have one identity or property but actually have a different identity or property. They claim that younger children are alert to the appearance-reality distinction in cases where the appearance is not initially deceptive. Thus, in the months before or after their third birthday, children begin to comment on the difference between a real as compared with a toy instance of a given category. A group of 3-year-olds marked this distinction under experimental conditions. In future studies, we plan to check how readily children can switch between a nonliteral (e.g., "ice cream") and a literal reference (e.g., "block"). Note that children were not asked to state the prop's real identity in Experiments 6 and 7.

A second limitation of Experiments 6 and 7 is that children were invited to talk about only pretend aspects of the physical world. For example, they were not called on to describe the psychological reactions of the animals to Teddy's mischief. Yet it is likely that 2-year-olds can imagine and describe simple psychological states in nonliteral terms. For example, we might expect 2-year-olds to be able to attribute goal-oriented actions to toy animals and dolls (e.g., "help," "chase," "hide"). Equally, we might expect the attribution of simple perceptual states ("see," "hear") and sensations ("hurt," "hungry"). A pioneering study by Wolf and her colleagues has shown that 2- and 3-year-olds can imagine and attribute pretend psychological states in the course of their spontaneous play with dolls (Wolf, Rygh, & Altshuler, 1984). On the basis of these observations, it has been proposed that the child's early conception of mind depends critically on this imaginative ability (Harris, 1989). The study of pretense comprehension rather than production offers an opportunity to test this claim much more systematically. For instance, 2-year-olds could be shown a small drama (e.g., a child doll who falls over; a mother doll who approaches and puts an arm around the child) and asked to describe it. The critical experimental question would be when and how children go beyond the literal facts (i.e., the bodily displacements of the two dolls) to attribute make-believe psychological sensations, states, and goals (e.g., "hurt," "sad," "help").

THE CHILD'S ENTRY INTO DRAMA AND FICTION

In conclusion, our results suggest that 2-year-olds are already alert to some of the critical components of drama and fiction. They recognize the existence of such make-believe worlds; they recognize that what takes place in a make-believe world respects, in part, the causal regularities of the real world while introducing unexpected deviations; and they can participate in the joint construction of a make-believe world. We consider each of these components in turn.

Our results show that children treat a pretend episode as conveying, not what is or might be true in the real world, but what takes place in a made-up or make-believe world. In replying to the adult's questions about what had happened, children described what had occurred in this make-believe world, not what had literally taken place. Recall that children's descriptions were rarely infected by real-world identities, as underlined in Experiment 7.

The causal construction of fictional or dramatic episodes presents a fascinating paradox. These episodes belong to a make-believe world that is cut off from the ordinary, real world. Within this make-believe world, it is possible to violate some of the empirical regularities that our everyday scripts, taxonomies, and folk theories prescribe. Such violations (albeit of a simple and innocuous variety) were deliberately introduced into the episodes of Experiments 5–7. At the same time, fiction and drama make tacit use of our knowledge of those same causal regularities. Even the peculiar worlds of pantomime, fairy stories, and science fiction presuppose certain familiar causal sequences. The constructive flagging process is well equipped to deal with this hybrid constitution. Each flag has only a limited force; it ceases to be read and obeyed once the pretend episode comes to an end. Thus, the flagging process reflects the circumscribed nature of the make-believe world. Yet, within such make-believe episodes, children can encounter events that are intriguing because, despite being parasitic on causal regularities in the real world, they lead to unexpected outcomes. To understand that toothpaste might be squeezed onto a banana or a pig's tail, children must continue to make use of their knowledge of causation in the real world. The flag-editing process offers an explanation for this type of incorporation.

Third, the constructive flagging process provides an explanation for the onset of genuinely social play. This form of play constitutes a type of collaborative drama or narrative. In constructing such a narrative, each partner uses general knowledge, previously supplied information, and the immediate context to extrapolate beyond the bare, or literal, meaning of the other partner's contribution. Similarly, the flagging process that we have described enables the child to make sense of a partner's pretend contribution and to respond appropriately within the pretense mode.

These various considerations suggest that the relation between pretense comprehension and the comprehension of text—particularly narrative text —may go beyond mere analogy. The child's ability to accept make-believe stipulations might provide a cognitive foundation not only for games of make-believe but also for responding to fiction and drama and possibly to works of art in general. This argument is speculative from a psychological point of view, but it gains strong support from recent philosophical analyses of the nature of fiction, drama, and painting. Currie (1990), for example, argues that the reader of fiction (as compared with nonfiction) "is invited by the author to engage in a game of make-believe, the structure of the game being in part dictated by the text of the author's work. What is said in the text, together with certain background assumptions, generates a set of fictional truths: those things that are true in the fiction" (p. 70). In a more wide-ranging analysis of the representational arts, Walton (1990) emphasizes the role of make-believe in our response to visual as well as textual representations. He suggests that paintings serve as elaborate props that guide viewers in a game of make-believe in which they imagine themselves seeing a mill, a seashore, or whatever is depicted in the painting. Both authors stress the continuity between an adult's response to works of art and children's participation in games of make-believe. Indeed, to the extent that they analyze works of art and the responses that they engender in terms of make-believe, the notion of make-believe assumes the role of a fundamental explanatory concept. As Currie explicitly acknowledges at the end of his examination of the nature of fiction, "One thing we could not have done without is the notion of make-believe, and that has remained stubbornly irreducible" (1990, p. 217).

These philosophical analyses highlight two exciting features of research on pretense comprehension. They reconfirm our earlier claim that the dominant theory of pretend play is too negative in its account of the long-term fate of the capacity for make-believe. Piaget emphasized that pretend play is a poor tool for the analysis of reality because children assimilate and distort reality when they engage in pretend play. Although this claim is narrowly correct, it ignores the fact that pretend play is aimed not at an analysis of reality but at the generation of make-believe truths. As children get older, they do not abandon the capacity for understanding and participating in games of make-believe—they continue to recruit that capacity throughout their lives whenever they read fiction, watch a film or play, or look at a painting. Early make-believe should not be seen simply as an intriguing cul-de-sac of cognitive development. An analysis of the child's ability to accept make-believe stipulations is foundational to an understanding of art and its impact throughout the life span.

Philosophical analyses have remained understandably silent about the cognitive processes that enter into adult responses to fiction, drama, or painting. Yet those analyses do suggest an important research strategy. Adult responses to works of art are obviously complex; they include a mixture of aesthetic and emotional concerns. If, however, we accept the philosophical claim that the capacity for make-believe is a key component in those diverse responses, we can profitably direct our attention to that component. The emergence of the child's ability to understand pretense is a good place to begin our analysis.

REFERENCES

Anderson, A., Garrod, S. C., & Sanford, A. J. (1983). The accessibility of pronominal antecedents as a function of episode shifts in narrative text. *Quarterly Journal of Experimental Psychology, 35A,* 427–440.

Astington, J. W., Harris, P. L., & Olson, D. R. (Eds.). (1988). *Developing theories of mind.* New York: Cambridge University Press.

Austin, J. L. (1962). *How to do things with words.* Cambridge, Mass.: Harvard University Press.

Avis, J., & Harris, P. L. (1991). Belief-desire reasoning among Baka children: Evidence for a universal conception of mind. *Child Development, 62,* 460–467.

Baron-Cohen, S., Leslie, A. M., & Frith, U. (1985). Does the autistic child have a theory of mind? *Cognition, 21,* 37–46.

Bates, E., Benigni, L., Bretherton, I., Camaione, L., & Volterra, J. (1979). *The emergence of symbols.* New York: Academic.

Bateson, G. (1972). *Steps to an ecology of mind.* New York: Chandler.

Bransford, J. D., & Johnson, M. K. (1972). Contextual prerequisites for understanding: Some investigations of comprehension and recall. *Journal of Verbal Learning and Verbal Behavior, 11,* 717–726.

Bretherton, I. (1984). Representing the social world in symbolic play: Reality and fantasy. In I. Bretherton (Ed.), *Symbolic play: The development of social understanding.* New York: Academic.

Bretherton, I., O'Connell, B., Shore, C., & Bates, E. (1984). The effect of contextual variation on symbolic play: Development from 20 to 28 months. In I. Bretherton (Ed.), *Symbolic play: The development of social understanding.* New York: Academic.

Brown, R., & Bellugi, U. (1964). Three processes in the child's learning of syntax. *Harvard Educational Review, 34,* 133–151. (Reprinted in R. Brown. [1970]. *Psycholinguistics.* New York: Free Press)

Chandler, M. (1988). Doubt and developing theories of mind. In J. W. Astington, P. L. Harris, & D. R. Olson (Eds.), *Developing theories of mind.* New York: Cambridge University Press.

Clark, E. V. (1983). Meanings and concepts. In J. H. Flavell & E. M. Markman (Eds.), P. H. Mussen (Series Ed.), *Handbook of child psychology: Vol. 3. Cognitive development.* New York: Wiley.

Currie, G. (1990). *The nature of fiction.* Cambridge: Cambridge University Press.

Dale, N. (1989). Pretend play with mothers and siblings: Relations between early performance and partners. *Journal of Child Psychology and Psychiatry, 30,* 751–759.

Das Gupta, P., & Bryant, P. E. (1989). Young children's causal inferences. *Child Development*, **60**, 1138–1146.

DeLoache, J. S., & Plaetzer, B. (1985, April). *Tea for two: Joint mother-child symbolic play.* Paper presented at the meeting of the Society for Research in Child Development, Toronto.

Dias, M., & Harris, P. L. (1990). The influence of the imagination on reasoning by young children. *British Journal of Developmental Psychology*, **8**, 305–318.

Dooling, D. J., & Lachman, R. (1971). Effects of comprehension on retention of prose. *Journal of Experimental Psychology*, **88**, 216–222.

Dunn, J., & Dale, N. (1984). I a Daddy: 2-year-olds' collaboration in joint pretend with sibling and with mother. In I. Bretherton (Ed.), *Symbolic play: The development of social understanding*. New York: Academic.

Estes, D., Wellman, H. M., & Woolley, J. D. (1989). Children's understanding of mental phenomena. In H. W. Reese (Ed.), *Advances in child development and behavior*. San Diego: Academic.

Fein, G. G. (1975). A transformational analysis of pretending. *Developmental Psychology*, **11**, 291–296.

Fein, G. G. (1981). Pretend play: An integrative review. *Child Development*, **52**, 1095–1118.

Fenson, L. (1984). Developmental trends for action and speech in pretend play. In I. Bretherton (Ed.), *Symbolic play: The development of social understanding*. New York: Academic.

Fenson, L., Dale, P. S., Reznick, J. S., Thal, D., Bates, E., Reilly, J. S., & Hartung, J. P. (1991, March). *Technical manual for the MacArthur Communicative Development Inventories: Preliminary version*. San Diego State University.

Fenson, L., & Ramsay, D. (1980). Decentration and integration of the child's play in the second year. *Child Development*, **51**, 171–178.

Fenson, L., & Ramsay, D. (1981). Effects of modeling actions on the play of twelve-, fifteen-, and nineteen-month-old children. *Child Development*, **52**, 1028–1036.

Fiese, B. H. (1988, April). *Come play with me: A longitudinal study of mother-toddler interaction and symbolic play.* Paper presented at the International Conference on Infant Studies, Washington, DC.

Fiese, B. H. (1990). Playful relationships: A contextual analysis of mother-child interaction and symbolic play. *Child Development*, **61**, 1648–1656.

Flavell, J. H. (1988). The development of children's knowledge about the mind: From cognitive connections to mental representations. In J. W. Astington, P. L. Harris, & D. R. Olson (Eds.), *Developing theories of mind*. New York: Cambridge University Press.

Fraser, C., Bellugi, U., & Brown, R. (1963). Control of grammar in imitation, comprehension, and production. *Journal of Verbal Learning and Verbal Behavior*, **2**, 121–135.

Garnham, A. (1981). Anaphoric reference to instances, instantiated and non-instantiated categories: A reading-time study. *British Journal of Psychology*, **72**, 377–384.

Garvey, C. (1984). *Children's talk*. London: Fontana.

Gelman, R., Bullock, M., & Meck, M. E. (1980). Preschoolers' understanding of simple object transformations. *Child Development*, **51**, 691–699.

Giffin, H. (1984). The coordination of meaning in the creation of a shared make-believe reality. In I. Bretherton (Ed.), *Symbolic play: The development of social understanding*. New York: Academic.

Givon, T. (1979). *On understanding grammar*. New York: Academic.

Goodman, N. (1976). *Languages of art*. Indianapolis: Hackett.

Harris, P. L. (1989). *Children and emotion*. Oxford: Blackwell.

Harris, P. L. (in press). Pretending and planning. In S. Baron-Cohen, H. Tager-Flusberg,

D. Cohen, & F. Volkmar (Eds.), *Understanding other minds: Perspectives from autism.* Oxford: Oxford University Press.

Harris, P. L., Brown, E., Marriott, C., Whittall, S., & Harmer, S. (1991). Monsters, ghosts and witches: Testing the limits of the fantasy-reality distinction. *British Journal of Developmental Psychology, 9,* 105–123.

Harris, P. L., Kavanaugh, R. D., & Walker-Andrews, A. (1990, August). *Reasoning from hypothetical premises.* Paper presented at the Fourth European Conference on Developmental Psychology, Stirling, Scotland.

Haviland, S. E., & Clark, H. H. (1974). What's new? Acquiring new information as a process in comprehension. *Journal of Verbal Learning and Verbal Behavior, 13,* 512–521.

Howes, C., Unger, O., & Seidner, L. B. (1989). Social pretend play in toddlers: Parallels with social play and with solitary pretend. *Child Development, 60,* 77–84.

Johnson, M. K., Bransford, J. D., & Solomon, S. (1973). Memory for tacit implications of sentences. *Journal of Experimental Psychology, 98,* 203–205.

Kavanaugh, R. D., & Harris, P. L. (1991, September). *Comprehension and production of pretend language by 2-year-olds.* Paper presented at the annual meeting of the Developmental Section, British Psychological Society, Cambridge.

Kavanaugh, R. D., Whittington, S., & Cerbone, M. J. (1983). Mother's use of fantasy in speech to young children. *Journal of Child Language, 10,* 45–55.

Lesgold, A., Roth, S., & Curtis, M. (1979). Foregrounding effects in discourse comprehension. *Journal of Verbal Learning and Verbal Behavior, 18,* 668–682.

Leslie, A. M. (1987). Pretense and representation: The origins of "theory of mind." *Psychological Review, 94,* 412–426.

Leslie, A. M. (1988a). The necessity of illusion: Perception and thought in infancy. In L. Weiskrantz (Ed.), *Thought without language.* Oxford: Oxford University Press.

Leslie, A. M. (1988b). Some implications of pretense for mechanisms underlying the child's theory of mind. In J. W. Astington, P. L. Harris, & D. R. Olson (Eds.), *Developing theories of mind.* New York: Cambridge University Press.

Lewis, V., & Boucher, J. (1988). Spontaneous, instructed and elicited play in relatively able autistic children. *British Journal of Developmental Psychology, 6,* 315–324.

Lillard, A. (1992). *Pretend play: Zone of proximal development or fool's gold?* Unpublished manuscript, University of San Francisco.

McCune-Nicolich, L. (1981). Toward symbolic functioning: Structure of early pretend games and potential parallels with language. *Child Development, 52,* 785–797.

McCune-Nicolich, L., & Fenson, L. (1984). Methodological issues in studying early pretend play. In T. D. Yawkey & A. D. Pellegrini (Eds.), *Child's play: Developmental and applied.* Hillsdale, NJ: Erlbaum.

Meltzoff, A. N. (1988). Infant imitation and memory: Nine-month-olds in immediate and deferred tests. *Child Development, 59,* 217–225.

Meltzoff, A. N., & Moore, M. K. (1983). The origins of imitation in infancy: Paradigm, phenomena, and theories. In L. P. Lipsitt (Ed.), *Advances in infancy research* (Vol. 2). Norwood, NJ: Ablex.

Miller, P., & Garvey, C. (1984). Mother-baby role play: Its origins in social support. In I. Bretherton (Ed.), *Symbolic play: The development of social understanding.* New York: Academic.

Mitchell, R. W. (1991). Bateson's concept of "metacommunication" in play. *New Ideas in Psychology, 9,* 73–87.

Morrow, D. G., Bower, G. H., & Greenspan, S. E. (1990). Situation-based inferences during narrative comprehension. In A. C. Graesser & G. H. Bower (Eds.), *Inferences and text comprehension: The psychology of learning and motivation* (Vol. 25). New York: Academic.

Myers, J. L., & Duffy, S. A. (1990). Causal inferences and text memory. In A. C. Graesser & G. H. Bower (Eds.), *Inferences and text comprehension: The psychology of learning and motivation* (Vol. **25**). New York: Academic.

Nelson, K. (1973). Structure and strategy in learning to talk. *Monographs of the Society for Research in Child Development,* **38**(1–2, Serial No. 149).

Nicolich, L. (1977). Beyond sensorimotor intelligence: Assessment of symbolic maturity through analysis of pretend play. *Merrill-Palmer Quarterly,* **23,** 89–99.

O'Connell, B., & Bretherton, I. (1984). Toddler's play, alone and with mother: The role of maternal guidance. In I. Bretherton (Ed.), *Symbolic play: The development of social understanding.* New York: Academic.

Olson, D. R., Astington, J. W., & Harris, P. L. (1988). Introduction. In J. W. Astington, P. L. Harris, & D. R. Olson (Eds.), *Developing theories of mind.* New York: Cambridge University Press.

Perner, J. (1991). *Understanding the representational mind.* Cambridge, Mass.: Bradford/MIT Press.

Perner, J. (in press). The theory of mind deficit in autism: Rethinking the metarepresentational theory. In S. Baron-Cohen, H. Tager-Flusberg, D. Cohen, & F. Volkmar (Eds.), *Understanding other minds: Perspectives from autism.* Oxford: Oxford University Press.

Piaget, J. (1951). *Play, dreams and imitation.* London: Heinemann.

Pinker, S. (1984). *Language learnability and language development.* Cambridge, Mass.: Harvard University Press.

Potts, G. R., Keenan, J. M., & Golding, J. M. (1988). Assessing the occurrence of elaborative inferences: Lexical decision versus naming. *Journal of Memory and Language,* **27,** 399–415.

Sachs, J. (1983). Talking about the there and then: The emergence of displaced reference in parent-child discourse. In K. E. Nelson (Ed.), *Children's language* (Vol. **4**). Hillsdale, NJ: Erlbaum.

Sanford, A. J., & Garrod, S. C. (1981). *Understanding written language.* New York: Wiley.

Saussure, F. de. (1983). *Course in general linguistics.* London: Duckworth. (Original work published 1916)

Schwartzmann, H. (1978). *Transformations: The anthropology of children's play.* New York: Plenum.

Slade, A. (1987a). A longitudinal study of maternal involvement and symbolic play during the toddler period. *Child Development,* **58,** 367–375.

Slade, A. (1987b). Quality of attachment and early symbolic play. *Developmental Psychology,* **23,** 78–85.

Sperber, D., & Wilson, D. (1986). *Relevance.* Oxford: Blackwell.

Trabasso, T., & Sperry, L. L. (1985). Causal relatedness and importance of story events. *Journal of Memory and Language,* **24,** 595–611.

Trabasso, T., & van den Broek, P. (1985). Causal thinking and the representation of narrative events. *Journal of Memory and Language,* **24,** 612–630.

Ungerer, J. A., Zelazo, P. R., Kearsley, R. B., & O'Leary, K. (1981). Developmental changes in the representation of objects in symbolic play from 18 to 34 months of age. *Child Development,* **52,** 186–195.

Walton, K. L. (1990). *Mimesis as make-believe.* Cambridge, Mass.: Harvard University Press.

Watson, M. W., & Fischer, K. W. (1977). A developmental sequence of agent use in late infancy. *Child Development,* **48,** 828–836.

Wellman, H. M. (1990). *The child's theory of mind.* Cambridge, Mass.: Bradford/MIT Press.

Wellman, H. M., & Estes, D. (1986). Early understanding of mental entities: A reexamination of childhood realism. *Child Development,* **57,** 910–923.

Wimmer, H., & Perner, J. (1983). Beliefs about beliefs: Representations and constraining function of wrong beliefs in young children's understanding of deception. *Cognition,* **13,** 103–128.

Wolf, D. P., Rygh, J., & Altshuler, J. (1984). Agency and experience: Actions and states in play narratives. In I. Bretherton (Ed.), *Symbolic play: The development of social understanding.* New York: Academic.

Woolley, J., & Wellman, H. M. (1990). Young children's understanding of realities, nonrealities, and appearances. *Child Development,* **61,** 946–961.

ACKNOWLEDGMENTS

We thank several colleagues who commented on earlier drafts of this manuscript, notably Simon Baron-Cohen, Carl Johnson, Angeline Lillard, Peter Mundy, Josef Perner, Arlene Walker-Andrews, and Henry Wellman. We also thank the reviewers for their constructive criticism. Gill Surman and many students helped gather the data, including Lucy Grey, Clare Mendham, Jo Sturgess, and Michelle Turner. Paul Harris was supported by a pump-priming grant from the University of Oxford and by a grant from the Economic and Social Research Council (U.K.) (R000 23 3543).

UNDERSTANDING PRETENSE AS PRETENSE

Henry M. Wellman and Anne K. Hickling

Children's engagement in and understanding of pretense is a classic topic in developmental research (e.g., Piaget, 1962), and for good reason. Pretend play emerges regularly in normally developing children; it emerges early, typically around 18 months of age, and then grows rapidly in complexity and frequency. A child is atypical indeed who does not spend many preschool hours engaged in pretense, sometimes alone, but most often with others. Like language acquisition, pretend play may be a universal, rapidly acquired human competence. But it is a peculiar and intriguing competence. In pretense, the child treats nothing as something (an empty pot as full of soup), treats one thing as something else (a block as a car or a house), and purposefully misreads actions and events (an empty cup raised to the face of an inanimate doll as a baby being fed). Much of the story of early cognitive development concerns, appropriately enough, the child's increasing competence at understanding the world "correctly," for example, coming to understand what physical objects are really like, what words conventionally refer to, how other people actually behave. In pretense, the child gets the story wrong, not by mistake, but by meaningfully construing things otherwise. Intriguingly, "this ability is not the sober culmination of intellectual development but instead makes its appearance playfully and precociously at the very beginning of childhood" (Leslie, 1987, p. 412).

Developmental psychologists' interest in pretense has risen yet another level with increasing realization of the significance of the child's *understanding* of pretense. When adults see a child pretend, we understand it as make-believe—the child is making believe that an alternative state of affairs exists, representing in both mind and action some hypothetical scenario. Children's understanding of their own and others' pretense may, therefore, imply that they can construe persons as "believing," "representing," and "hypothesizing," that is, engaging in various mental activities. If so, early engagement in and understanding of pretense suggests a dramatically early understanding of mind. However, we actually know very little about children's understanding of pretense, as most research concerns children's production of pretense instead. What do young children, who engage in pretense, understand about pretense, and what does that tell us about their cognition and conception?

The great attraction of the Harris and Kavanaugh *Monograph* is that they begin to tackle this question systematically and empirically. To do so, they confront sizable difficulties: the paucity of established research tasks, the difficulties of testing such very young children at all, and myriad alternative explanations for children's apparent understanding. In spite of the difficulties, they achieve some remarkable successes. They provide us with seven systematic studies, an informative interpretation of their specific findings and of early pretense more broadly, detailed comparisons to alternative accounts, and suggestions for further intriguing research.

Part of the reason for the success of their efforts is their adoption and development of a particular theoretical stance toward children's pretense comprehension. Their findings are interpreted within, provide support for, and help develop a construal of pretense comprehension as deeply akin to the processes required to comprehend written or spoken text. Harris and Kavanaugh make this theoretical stance an intriguing and compelling hypothesis. Both pretense comprehension and text comprehension require the comprehender to engage in constructive inference making, filling various gaps in a presentation to arrive at a coherent mental representation. Harris and Kavanaugh tackle children's abilities to make the needed inferences and extensions, to construct sensible representations of scenarios where referents are missing, imprecisely specified, and not real. Moreover, they use aspects of what is known about text comprehension processes to begin to sketch a process model for early pretense comprehension—their "flagging" model. They use the analogy to reorient us helpfully to the developmental trajectory and power of pretense skills and suggest forcefully that pretense marks the child's appropriate entry into the world of fiction and drama, rather than the child's failures to deal appropriately with conventional symbol systems such as language.

This theoretical orientation helps us focus our Commentary just as it helps Harris and Kavanaugh focus their research and interpretations. In our opinion, the basic analogy between pretense comprehension and text comprehension inspires many of the strengths of the *Monograph*, and it supports some impressive conclusions. For example, if the analogy is sound, then not only does consideration of text processing tell us about pretense, but analyses of pretense also reveal some of the child's early competences at text processing. After all, Harris and Kavanaugh demonstrate aspects of pretense comprehension achieved by 2-year-olds well before children evince later story and text comprehension skills. But this theoretical orientation also poses some challenges; theoretical commitments both support and constrain research.

One feature of considerable importance in many accounts of text comprehension concerns the sort of text to be comprehended: is it a fictional story, a real-life biography, technical instructions, directions to do something? Harris and Kavanaugh are mostly silent about how and when children might distinguish between various kinds of text, for example, pretense versus instructions. They are more concerned with similarities in comprehension processes across such different texts: text processing in general, according to this analysis, requires interpreting and keeping track of complex referential relations (including statements about entities that are not now present or viewable but must be imagined), filling in the gaps to construct an integrated overall representation, and updating such a representation on the basis of new information. For example, consider the written instructions for the assembly of some newly purchased equipment, a bookshelf, say, or a child's swing set. Such instructions are rarely exhaustively complete, and some instructions transliterated from other languages may require considerable comprehension skills indeed. The comprehender's task in such a case is still to make certain references ("part A" means this thing), envision certain imaginary or hypothetical states of affairs (what the object will look like once assembled, although no such assembled object is now available), and infer what certain instructions must mean, even if the words are foreign or missing or unclear.

This instruction-following example, encompassed by Harris and Kavanaugh's own analogy, poses some concerns for the interpretation of their experiments and results. Most important, in their research, children could conceivably perform correctly via general text comprehension processes without an understanding of pretense *as pretense*. To perform correctly, children would have demonstrated impressive abilities at inferential comprehension of difficult texts. But, beyond simply following deviant references and complex transformations and thereby achieving some sensible understanding of what they are being instructed to do, an essential question that these studies hope to and should address is whether children understand pretense as pretense—as referring to an alternative realm of fictional identities, actions, and consequences.

Take Experiment 1 as an example. Perhaps children do not treat the adult's request as pretense, a possibility the authors admit. One way in which that might happen is the one they describe: children might simply be cued to use the props normally. The experimental design helps defeat this "selective cuing" hypothesis. But what if the children are just trying to treat the requests as serious directions and listen to essentially only the key phrase "give tea/cereal." Without any pretense, what would children do? It seems likely that, in one instance, they would give the teapot and, in the other, the cereal box. If so, how do we know that the behavior reported is pretense, rather than just constructive instruction following? It is true that there is no "real tea" or "real cereal." But there is an obvious teapot and cereal bowl, and, in the warm-up, children have been instructed to treat phrases of the form "give the toy [e.g., the elephant] some referent [e.g., milk]" as an instruction to take a prop associated with the referent (a glass or a milk carton) and put it to the toy animal's face. In the experimental task, children might simply follow the same instructions, filling in the necessary slots, without understanding the presentation as pretense or their actions as an extension of the pretense.

The situation is similar for Experiment 2. In the warm-up, the child is instructed to refer to the yellow bricks as "bananas" and the red bricks as "cake" and is further instructed that, in this context, "giving banana" or "cake" means taking a brick from the appropriate pile (and not a previously used brick) and presenting it to the animal. In the experimental phase, perhaps children simply continue to follow these special instructions. Note the similarity and the difference of this sort of alternative explanation to Harris and Kavanaugh's preferred interpretation. The similarity is that such a process of constructive instruction following requires understanding stipulated references and then filling in gaps. Following instructions in this interpretation is far from simple and requires some complex cognitive capacities to follow special referential stipulations; just the sort of comprehension required in our earlier example about written instructions (call this thing— which is clearly a board—"part A," or "the seat," or "the foot"). The difference in the two interpretations, therefore, is that such instruction following does not require an understanding of pretense. To make this distinction clearer, consider the complement to the above examples. In the above discussion, we contemplate a child who follows all the transformations and stipulations but fails to understand that it is pretense. Now consider a child who fails to follow all the complications and thus fails to understand the "story" but who still adopts the appropriate interpretation that the scenario is pretend, a playful, nonserious, fictional state of affairs, albeit one that he or she does not understand. Children demonstrate some intriguing abilities to follow complex stipulations in the current studies, but do they understand them to be pretense stipulations or, instead, some other sort of stipulation?

This concern, which follows from Harris and Kavanaugh's own framework, is different from the alternative explanations that they contend with and dispel (word learning, associated props, and selective cuing). One way in which other studies of pretense deal with this and related concerns is by reporting data not only about children's successful behaviors but also indicating their attitudes about the pretense. That young children often see such scenarios and situations as pretense seems evident in cases where they exhibit "knowing smiles," playful executions, and exaggerated actions. Such data would have been useful in the current research and seem an important addition to the authors' agenda of needed future research. Moreover, we suspect, as the authors themselves imply, that it may well prove more difficult for young children to follow instructions as a sequence of merely stipulated directions than it would be for them to understand and extend a stipulated pretend scenario. If so, it would be substantively and methodologically useful in future research for the authors directly to contrast pretense conditions with some instruction-following conditions that involve similar but more serious stipulations.

Beyond knowing smiles, children's understanding of pretense as pretense can be demonstrated in their language. For example, children can say that "it's pretend" or "not for real" (Woolley & Wellman, 1990). In this regard, Harris and Kavanaugh provide us with some important evidence. There are no data in the present studies as to children's parenthetical comments that "it's pretend," but, in Experiments 6 and 7, children must describe pretend scenarios. Correct responding in this case requires more than following instructions because the child must do more than perform an appropriate action. In their descriptions, children share their representations of the tasks. If children understand these tasks only as complex instruction-following situations, they might decode instructions such as "Give the monkey some tea" as "Put the teacup to the monkey's face." If asked, they might even describe such an act as "giving the monkey tea," reiterating the experimenter's own word. But, under this hypothesis, children would not have construed the scenario as a complex pretend event. If they have not, then there should be no basis and no reason for them to amplify further a pretend description of the scenario with appropriate fictional statements like "His mouth will be wet" or "Yum, yum, he thinks it's good tea." Experiments 6 and 7 show that 2-year-olds' extended descriptions of the presentations are voiced in the language of pretense, rather than in the language of instructions. With minimal questioning, children provide additional descriptions of the events that continue the pretense identities and actions, often with completely new terms and expressions, rather than providing literal descriptions or mere translations of the adults' stipulations.

Why raise this concern about the research if, in the end, we believe that the findings are resistant to such an alternative interpretation? We do so in part to highlight a nonobvious strength of the research. But, in addition, dispelling this concern requires something of a reinterpretation of the nature of the findings. For example, Harris and Kavanaugh tend to interpret their experiments individually, as each isolating and confirming the presence of various aspects of the pretend comprehension process: "From the results of Experiment 1, we know that children interpret a reference to a nonexistent object as a make-believe stipulation of that object rather than as a deviant utterance" (p. 61); or, "Experiment 5 showed that children understand pretend transformations whose outcomes are invisible" (p. 58). Our interpretation is somewhat different; many of the studies taken singly raise as many questions as answers, but, nonetheless, a compelling pattern of results emerges over the sequence of studies taken together. This sort of interpretation, if accepted, places some definite constraints on the overall conclusions that can be accepted. In particular, it seems to us that the current studies provide the needed cumulative evidence only for those children who consistently perform appropriately, 2-year-olds. There are no demonstrations, such as those provided in Experiments 6 and 7 for older children, that before the age of 2 years children understand the experimenter's stipulations as pretense. There is little if any evidence in Experiments 3 and 4 that 1½-year-olds even understand multiple stipulated identities. We are uncomfortable, therefore, concluding that the research has demonstrated pretense understanding before age 2. More generally, in spite of the authors' hopes, it seems to us that the results tell us little about the development of pretense understanding; they more conservatively establish the presence and something of the nature of that understanding by the time children reach the third year of life. This is a great deal, although not quite as much as the authors lay claim to. Note, for example, that 2-year-olds' competences, as demonstrated here, are sufficiently extensive that they strongly suggest some informative understanding of pretense at still earlier ages. It should now be possible to demonstrate something of the nature of this understanding and to paint a clearer developmental picture.

There is a deeper aspect of Harris and Kavanaugh's theoretical commitment to viewing pretense comprehension as analogous to text comprehension that deserves comment. Harris and Kavanaugh concentrate on the pretend episode itself as a text—an objective scenario that must be understood by the observant, comprehending child. But, as argued above, the child's task is not just to understand the scenario but, crucially, to understand it as pretense. Children must understand that the other is adopting a special construal of, or attitude toward, the events portrayed. Further, children should themselves adopt an attitude of pretense. This is a point that Leslie (1987) emphasizes; pretending that something is the case is similar to mental attitudes such as believing that something is the case. Minimally, in both believing and pretending, there is someone who has an attitude—believing or pretending—about a state of affairs. Harris and Kavanaugh contend that children need not understand this attitude in order to understand pretense: "We anticipate that children might be able to engage in pretense . . . without diagnosing the mental state of their play partner or of themselves" (p. 76). Perhaps, to pursue an example that Harris has used elsewhere (Harris, 1991), the child is like a playgoer understanding a drama. The child need not understand that the actors are pretending; he need only understand the play as a text. In this case, understanding pretense would involve nothing more than keeping track of objects' stipulated identities and the transformations performed on them. This is just what Harris and Kavanaugh suggest and what they study.

But this raises some serious questions. Not the least of the questions is, Are Harris and Kavanaugh correct? Do young children merely comprehend the pretend text without any understanding of the pretenders' special relation to or attitude toward the text? This is an empirical question, although the *Monograph* does not tackle it. At the least, this seems an important omission. Regardless of theoretical commitments, when children understand what about the pretenders' special relations to the pretense seems a central question for the investigation of children's understanding of pretense. Moreover, for Harris and Kavanaugh this constitutes a crucial theoretical hypothesis that needs to be tested. Note that children need not at first understand "pretending" as an attitude equivalent to "believing" but may still understand something essential about it.

In the absence of any data, there are reasons to suspect that young children may know more about pretending than Harris and Kavanaugh believe and that an emphasis on pretend scenarios solely as texts may be misleading. A pretender not only acts a part but also creates it. The pretender's role seems more like those of the writer, the director, and the actor combined than simply an animate prop with a stipulated identity. As the writer/creator, pretenders adopt a certain stance toward their actions; they take them to be fiction, exaggerate or stage them in certain fashions, and engage in knowing smiles. Like the director, pretenders give stage directions: "You be the Mommy"; "Give Teddy something to drink." In pretense, children observe more than an objectively unfolding text; they observe persons engaged in subjective reactions and attitudes toward the text: creating it, directing it, treating it fictionally, not simply presenting it. Moreover, the child's role is rarely that of a passive observer—a playgoer. He or she is more typically an active participant in the shaping and creating of the pretense episode. Pretense occurs in a social-interactive context, and this gives children special information as to their own stance toward the episode and, hence, the mental attitude of at least one agent toward the props and events. Thus, the subjects, child and other, and not just the objective text, form an integral part of pretense. In comprehending pretense, what children make of the players and their attitudes toward the events, not only how they follow the pretend events, may be essential. To reiterate, these aspects of understanding pretense deserve research; they are central to the authors' topic: children's understanding of pretense. As we see it, the needed research goes beyond Harris and Kavanaugh's suggestion that they investigate young children's understanding of pretend psy-chological states—understanding that Teddy may be unhappy or curious as well as wet. Equally important would be an examination of children's understanding of the *players'* mental state of pretense.

As one example here consider that, if children concentrate on the text itself, with no regard to the persons' attitudes of pretense, this should lead to certain telltale errors. At some early age, for example, children should incorrectly attribute the fictions involved in the pretense to the props and situations, as opposed to the players. According to Harris and Kavanaugh, fictional flags are planted on the props themselves. If so, at some appro-priate age children should misunderstand what a new person, just entering the pretense, would know and do. If the fiction exists in the text, then it is there for anyone to read or comprehend. If, instead, it is a crucial attitude on the part of the players, then only those who have adopted this attitude can be expected to act appropriately. As a sketch of how these questions and contrasting positions could be studied, a task similar to those used to assess false belief understanding could be used to investigate what beliefs about pretend identities children expect newcomers to an episode to hold. Children could be asked to stipulate a new identity for a prop while a player is absent from the room and then to predict what identity the returning player will attribute to the prop. More generally, studies of this sort could reveal the extent to which children are and are not sensitive to players' mental states of pretense and to the conditions of knowledge formation within a pretend episode.

Finally, we wish to comment briefly on Harris and Kavanaugh's outline of a process model for pretense comprehension, their "flagging" proposal. The flagging model has several attractions on its own, and, in addition, it is extremely helpful to have an alternative to Leslie's (1987) decoupling model. Assessing the relative virtues of Harris and Kavanaugh's flagging model and Leslie's decoupling model presents no easy task, however. At one level, the mechanisms involved in the two models appear strikingly similar, an affinity acknowledged by Harris and Kavanaugh. Both models are directed at describing how a cognitive system can quarantine pretend construals ("Teddy is wet") from literal construals ("Teddy is dry") in order to avoid representational abuse, the overextension of pretend claims to the real world. Given this similarity, it is tempting to discount certain differences as primarily semantic ones. Decoupled expressions anchored to current per-ceptual representations, to use Leslie's words, begin to sound a lot like labeled flags attached to a specific prop, to use Harris and Kavanaugh's words. There are, however, some real differences worth pursuing. We have already discussed one of these, the extent to which each model conceptual-izes pretense as involving awareness of the players' relationship to the pre-tense. On this point, we find it an attraction of Leslie's model that it emphasizes the role of particular agents as they relate to pretend states of affairs. This difference in the models can be subjected to empirical test.

At a different level, Harris and Kavanaugh suggest that a key difference between the flagging and the decoupling models is the direction in which their mechanisms operate. Flagging begins by considering the pretend stipulation, a fictional representation directed toward a prop within an episode, whereas decoupling begins by considering the prop as literally represented, then altering a copy of the literal representation to achieve a pretend representation. Harris and Kavanaugh suggest that, by beginning with a decoupled copy of the literal representation, Leslie's model suffers from a deletion problem. If the target prop is literally "a small broken empty cup," for example, the initial pretend representation will contain extraneous ("broken"), even contradictory ("empty") features that must somehow be appropriately pruned or interpreted to achieve the needed pretend representation ("This cup holds tea"). Leslie is silent about the needed deletions, and they may well prove a serious problem, one that the flagging model sidesteps by beginning instead with the pretend stipulation itself ("This cup hold tea").

By beginning in the opposite direction, however, Harris and Kavanaugh may have to contend with the complementary problem, which we will call the "importation problem." In the sorts of situations studied by Harris and Kavanaugh, the child is shown a prop, say a cup, and told, for example, to "give Teddy some tea." Harris and Kavanaugh suggest that a flag is written such as "This cup holds tea" and attached to the episode. But why and how is the pretend stipulation, the flag, written as "This cup holds tea"? Why not "This object *is* tea," leading to boiling it in water, or "This broken cup can't hold tea," leading to mending the cup. That is, how does the child decide which features of the real prop to import, and which not, into the pretend stipulation (its identity as a cup rather than simply an object, the fact that it is broken). Importing the proper literal features into the pretense may be a problem for the flagging model, just as deleting the irrelevant literal features from the pretense may be for the decoupling model. We look forward to the authors' further development and articulation of their model and to a response by Leslie as well.

Although we have expressed some concerns, advanced some reinterpretations, and pointed out what we see as a major untackled issue, the *Monograph* stands as a major achievement. Harris and Kavanaugh tackle an important but almost unstudied topic, young children's understanding of pretense, in a systematic and informative fashion. The work is lucid and articulate, a pleasure to read and think about, a text well worth comprehending. So much remains unknown, perhaps surprisingly, on this topic that the research cannot and does not claim to be definitive or exhaustive. However, it sets an impressive standard, charting phenomena, methods, and theory that establish an important foundation for further research and debate.

References

Harris, P. L. (1991). The work of the imagination. In A. Whiten (Ed.), *Natural theories of mind.* Oxford: Basil Blackwell.

Leslie, A. M. (1987). Pretense and representation: The origins of "theory of mind." *Psychological Review,* **94,** 412–426.

Piaget, J. (1962). *Play, dreams, and imitation in childhood.* London: Routledge & Kegan Paul.

Woolley, J., & Wellman, H. M. (1990). Young children's understanding of realities, nonrealities, and appearances. *Child Development,* **61,** 946–961.

THE RIGHT ATTITUDE?

Paul L. Harris and Robert D. Kavanaugh

We thank Henry Wellman and Anne Hickling for their praise and constructive criticism. Their commentary prompts us to think afresh about our findings but also leads us to reaffirm our original theoretical commitments. We begin with the latter.

Wellman and Hickling take us to task because we emphasize the child's understanding of a pretend episode and ignore the question of whether children understand the pretender's "special relation or attitude" to the pretend episode. Allegedly, we contend that children "need not understand this attitude in order to understand pretense." Wellman and Hickling misrepresent us, however. We did not claim that children can get by with *no* understanding of the pretender's relation to the pretend episode. Rather, we argued that 2-year-olds might have a restricted understanding of the nature of pretense. Specifically, they might understand much about pretense—including the pretender's special relation or attitude—by construing it as a special form of action rather than as a distinctive mental state.

A pretend action such as "drinking" from an empty cup or "eating" a wooden block is special because the agent acts on imaginary or substitute objects rather than actual objects. A child who construes an agent as drinking make-believe tea is necessarily interpreting that agent as doing something different from drinking real tea. In that sense, our theoretical model commits us to the claim that 2-year-olds recognize the pretender as engaged in a distinct form of activity when he or she pretends. We make this point quite explicitly in discussing the theoretical proposals of both Leslie and Perner. In particular, we argue that children can identify particular agents performing actions in relation to props that have a specific make-believe status.

Notice that a child who understands pretending as a special form of activity is well placed to grasp the various features of pretending eloquently highlighted by Wellman and Hickling—its potential for creative, active collaboration. We happily acknowledge that these deserve further investigation. Indeed, we hope that our studies of comprehension will, in combination with earlier work on production, serve as a fillip to the study of joint play. A we pointed out, successful joint play necessarily involves the coordination of production with comprehension on the part of each player. Still, we insist that an investigation of joint play, especially by 2-year-olds, would not require and would not amount to an investigation of children's understanding of pretense as a mental state.

Admittedly, as adults, we recognize that pretending is not just a special form of activity. It also involves specific types of mental representation. For example, pretending to drink tea requires that the pretender (a) has some conception of what tea is and (b) imagines it in the cup that he or she "drinks" from. A pretender who lifts a cup to his or her lips, but has no conception of what tea is, or imagines that the cup contains gin and tonic, is not pretending to drink tea. An understanding of these mental prerequisites, however, is not critical to an understanding of pretense. Thus, we argued that 2-year-olds can understand a player as performing a pretend action without recognizing that certain mental representations must underpin that action.

There are three sources of evidence that support our claim. First, even school-aged children do not systematically assert that the mind is needed to engage in simple activities such as walking or talking (Johnson & Wellman, 1982, study 2). Second, 4- and 5-year-olds do not reliably acknowledge the necessary role of mental representations for pretend actions (Lillard, in press). Third, preliminary evidence shows that 3- and 4-year-olds make errors consistent with a neglect of the role of mental representation: they fail to take into account what a player does and does not know about the current make-believe situation (Freeman, 1992). We know of no evidence concerning 2-year-olds, but it seems unlikely that they would appreciate what older children do not.

In sum, Wellman and Hickling chide us for ignoring the special relation between pretender and pretend situation. We did not ignore that relationship; we claimed that 2-year-olds construe it in terms of a special form of activity. Research with older children supports our claim and provides little support for the proposal introduced by Leslie (1987)—and echoed by Wellman and Hickling—that 2-year-olds understand pretense as involving a special form of mental representation.

We turn now to Wellman and Hickling's important and provocative comment on textual genres. They note that texts are of various types and argue that some are fictional and some instructional. We propose that 2-

year-olds have a competence akin to that needed for text processing. Hence, we attribute considerable power to the 2-year-old. Wellman and Hickling's cautionary point is that we may have attributed too general a competence— one that might enable the child to treat the pretend episode as a set of instructions rather than as a piece of make-believe. This alternative inter-pretation is, they assert, especially feasible for children younger than 2 years of age because they were not included in Experiments 6 and 7 and therefore did not offer the more persuasive verbal replies that were recorded in those studies.

We maintain (a) that the relation between an instructional text and a fictional text is more complex than Wellman and Hickling allow and (b) that children in Studies 1–5, including those younger than 2 years, did approach the episodes as pretend episodes, not as a set of literal instructions.

The ad hoc props of pretense play often require an accompanying stipulation from a player if they are to serve a make-believe function. Thus, a player who says, "Let's give Teddy some banana," while holding a yellow block to Teddy's mouth is effectively instructing fellow players that the block is to count as a banana. During a pretend episode, one player may also give explicit instructions to another player to engage in a particular pretend action. For example, in Experiment 1, children were instructed to give the animal either tea or cereal. To comply, they needed to act appropri-ately on the correct prop.

Thus, Wellman and Hickling set up a dichotomy that is too simple when they distinguish between instructional and fictional texts. A pretend episode can contain tacit instructions (what we refer to as "stipulations"); it can also contain explicit instructions, albeit ones that are directed at the make-believe rather than the literal situation. The implication of these re-marks is that a child who complies with instructions is not, ipso facto, failing to pretend. Rather, we must consider the manner in which the child com-plies. In particular, we need to ask whether the child produces a pretend action that respects the make-believe situation that has been created or produces an ordinary motor action ignoring that make-believe situation.

Consider Experiment 1, in which children were asked to give the animal tea or cereal. Wellman and Hickling suggest that children may have re-sponded to such instructions literally—treating them as serious directions rather than as a request to give pretend tea or cereal. We find this suggestion implausible. Even the younger children (who were younger than 2 years) typically lifted the appropriate empty container (either a cup or a bowl and spoon) toward the animal's mouth in response to this instruction. Lifting an empty container toward the mouth is not a standard response to a request to give tea or cereal. Nor could the response have been based on simple model-ing. In the warm-up phase, the experimenter fed the animal from a differ-ent container (a glass), thereby offering no clue to the correct choice of container in the test phase. Nor is it likely that children acted selectively on the containers because of their differential asssociation with tea versus cereal. Had they chosen on the basis of association, then the teapot and the cereal carton would have offered stronger cues, yet children appropriately fed the animal from the cup or bowl and spoon. They did not hand the animal the teapot or the cereal carton, as Wellman and Hickling suggest. When children did act on the teapot or the cereal carton, it was to engage in pretend pouring. In sum, we readily agree that our subjects complied with the experimenter's instructions, but, in doing so, they respected the make-believe situation: they pretended that the relevant container held tea or cereal and "poured" or "fed" from it, as appropriate.

Wellman and Hickling acknowledge that the linguistic responses of Experiments 6 and 7 are especially persuasive. However, they ignore the equally important fact that children who participated in the earlier experiments needed to interpret the experimenter's verbal instructions in a nonliteral fashion if they were to respond correctly. Consider Experiment 5 in this light: the experimenter asked children to clean or dry an animal or a part of the floor that was dirty or wet. Had children tried to follow this instruction literally, they would have been unable to choose between the two pigs or between the two sides of the floor; in each case, these were clean and dry. Thus, the experimenter's instruction could be followed only selectively if it was interpreted in the light of the immediately preceding pretend action (the pouring of a make-believe substance from a familiar container).

Admittedly, when considered as a group, the younger children aged 18–24 months performed poorly in this experiment. However, a sizable minority (40%) made no response throughout the experiment. Among the remainder who did respond, all responded in a predominantly correct fashion. These results testify to the clear continuity between the competence of the children younger than 2 years, which we assessed using nonverbal responses, and the competence of the 2-year-olds, which we assessed using verbal replies.

In sum, we find Wellman and Hickling's alternative interpretation of our findings for children younger than 2 years implausible. It rests on too sharp a dichotomy between fictional and instructional input, and it fails to do justice to the rich competence that we observed.

Finally, we turn to the comparison between our theoretical proposals and those made by Leslie (1987). Wellman and Hickling make the important point that, whenever a pretend stipulation is encoded by a player, the mapping between the available props and the make-believe state is far from straightforward. Any given prop will have countless features ("cup"/ "chipped"/"white"/"empty" etc.). How does the child know which features of a given prop to import into a pretend stipulation? In line with our top-down orientation, we would argue that the child starts with the pretend request (e.g., "Give the pig some tea") and scans the environment for props with which to realize that request. We assume that there is a general principle of economy at work in the selection of a given realization. The child is parsimonious; literal features of the prop are exploited whenever they serve the make-believe situation that the child seeks to realize. As a result, flags may be brief and few in number. So the child is likely to comply with a request to offer tea by pretending that a cup or a teapot preserves its normal identity but contains make-believe tea. The child does not adopt the more imaginative but profligate solution of pretending that the cup is a tea bag and the teapot a saucepan containing hot water.

The results of our experiments strongly suggest that such a principle of parsimony does operate. Consider Experiment 1 once again. Children had various props at their disposal: a cup and teapot on one side, a cereal box, spoon, and bowl on the other side. Had children been indifferent to the objective identity of the props—for example, had they been equally willing to treat the teapot or the cereal carton as containers holding make-believe tea—then we would not have observed the selectivity that children actually displayed.

Nevertheless, we acknowledge that our response to Wellman and Hickling's helpful challenge requires further elaboration. We have used an intuitive notion of "parsimony," conveyed, we hope, by our examples. In the future, it will be important to provide a more explicit metric for the imaginative steps that are needed to comply with a pretend request. In that fashion, we should be able to track the developing power of the child's imagination in a more rigorous fashion. We thank Henry Wellman and Anne Hickling for keeping our eyes firmly on that long-term goal.

References

Freeman, N. (1992). *Facts and fictions in preschoolers' theory of mind: "Wrong pretense" and false belief.* Paper presented at the meeting of Association of Child Psychology and Psychiatry, Bristol, U.K., January.

Johnson, C. N., & Wellman, H. M. (1982). Children's developing conceptions of the mind and brain. *Child Development, 53,* 222–234.

Leslie, A. M. (1987). Pretense and representation: The origins of "theory of mind." *Psychological Review, 94,* 412–426.

Lillard, A. (in press). Young children's conceptualization of pretense: Action or mental representational state. *Child Development.*

CONTRIBUTORS

Paul L. Harris (D.Phil. 1971, University of Oxford) is university lecturer in psychology at the University of Oxford and fellow of St. John's College. His interests include the development of emotion and imagination. He is the author of *Children and Emotion* (1989).

Robert D. Kavanaugh (Ph.D. 1974, Boston University) is Hales Professor of Psychology at Williams College. His research focuses on language, pretend play, and symbolic thought.

Henry M. Wellman (Ph.D. 1975, University of Minnesota) is professor of psychology at the University of Michigan. His research interests include children's developing understanding of person's minds, including their understanding of mental states such as beliefs, desires, imagination, and emotions. His publications include *The Child's Theory of Mind* (1990).

Anne K. Hickling (A.B. 1989, Stanford University) is a doctoral candidate at the University of Michigan. Her research interests include early causal reasoning in the domains of biology and physics, the influence of magical and fantasy beliefs on children's causal explanations, and children's conception of imagination and pretense.

STATEMENT OF EDITORIAL POLICY

The *Monographs* series is intended as an outlet for major reports of developmental research that generate authoritative new findings and use these to foster a fresh and/or better-integrated perspective on some conceptually significant issue or controversy. Submissions from programmatic research projects are particularly welcome; these may consist of individually or group-authored reports of findings from some single large-scale investigation or of a sequence of experiments centering on some particular question. Multiauthored sets of independent studies that center on the same underlying question can also be appropriate; a critical requirement in such instances is that the various authors address common issues and that the contribution arising from the set as a whole be both unique and substantial. In essence, irrespective of how it may be framed, any work that contributes significant data and/or extends developmental thinking will be taken under editorial consideration.

Submissions should contain a minimum of 80 manuscript pages (including tables and references); the upper limit of 150–175 pages is much more flexible (please submit four copies; a copy of every submission and associated correspondence is deposited eventually in the archives of the SRCD). Neither membership in the Society for Research in Child Development nor affiliation with the academic discipline of psychology are relevant; the significance of the work in extending developmental theory and in contributing new empirical information is by far the most crucial consideration. Because the aim of the series is not only to advance knowledge on specialized topics but also to enhance cross-fertilization among disciplines or subfields, it is important that the links between the specific issues under study and larger questions relating to developmental processes emerge as clearly to the general reader as to specialists on the given topic.

Potential authors who may be unsure whether the manuscript they are planning would make an appropriate submission are invited to draft an outline of what they propose and send it to the Editor for assessment.

This mechanism, as well as a more detailed description of all editorial policies, evaluation processes, and format requirements, is given in the "Guidelines for the Preparation of *Monographs* Submissions," which can be obtained by writing to Wanda C. Bronson, Institute of Human Development, 1203 Tolman Hall, University of California, Berkeley, CA 94720.

NOTICE TO CONTRIBUTORS

As of August 1, 1993, manuscripts and inquiries should be directed to the Editor designate, Rachel K. Clifton, Department of Psychology, University of Massachusetts, Amherst, MA 01003. Current editorial policies will remain unchanged.